When Did ...

Become a Game of

Twister?

Other Books by Mary Pierce

When Did I Stop Being Barbie and Become Mrs. Potato Head?

Confessions of a Prayer Wimp

When Did My Life Become a Game of Twister?

Mary Pierce

ZONDERVAN®

ZONDERVAN.com/
AUTHORTRACKER
follow your favorite authors

When Did My Life Become a Game of Twister?
Copyright © 2007 by Mary Pierce

Requests for information should be addressed to:
Zondervan, *Grand Rapids, Michigan 49530*

Library of Congress Cataloging-in-Publication Data

Pierce, Mary.
    When did my life become a game of Twister? / Mary Pierce.
      p. cm.
    ISBN-13: 978-0-310-27237-3
    ISBN-10: 0-310-27237-8
    1. Women—Psychology. 2. Women—Conduct of life. 3. Christian life. I. Title.
HQ1206.P514 2007
155.3'33—dc22
                               2007013734

All Scripture quotations, unless otherwise indicated, are taken from the *Holy Bible, New International Version*®. NIV®. Copyright © 1973, 1978, 1984 by International Bible Society. Used by permission of Zondervan. All rights reserved.

Scripture quotations marked NLT are taken from the *Holy Bible*, New Living Translation, copyright © 1996. Used by permission of Tyndale House Publishers, Inc. Wheaton, Illinois, 60189.

Scripture quotations marked KJV are taken from the King James Version of the Bible.

Published in association with the literary agency of Alive Communications, Inc., 7680 Goddard Street, Suite 200, Colorado Springs, CO 80920.

Interior design by Beth Shagene

Printed in the United States of America

07 08 09 10 11 12 13 • 22 21 20 19 18 17 16 15 14 13 12 11 10 9 8 7 6 5 4 3 2 1

To Terry
Together. Forever.

Contents

Acknowledgments 9

Introduction 11

Part 1
The Game Begins

1. Twisted Sister 17

2. The Ideal Woman 27

3. High-Maintenance Woman 37

4. So Much Advice 47

5. Wake-up Call 55

6. My Eyelashes Hurt 63

Part 2
All Twisted Up

7. All Twisted Up 75

8. Let's Get Personal 85

9. Today the Sweatshirts 95

10. Kaflooey 105

11. A New Atti-toot 113

12. Of Mice and Women 123

13. I've Got It Coming 133

14. Temper, Temper 141

15. The Blame Game 151

16. Traffic Jams 161

Part 3
Untwisting the Knots

17. I Would If I Could 171

18. Wedding Whine 181

19. Better Questions, Better Answers . . . 189

20. My Toy Is Missing 201

21. Frames 211

22. Seeing 221

23. I Will Pass This Way but Once 229

Acknowledgments

Thanks to Mother, for still being here and for blessing us so. Thanks to the children, Alex, Katy, Lizz, Jenny, Laura, Dan, and mates—cheerleaders all. Thank you for letting me tell your stories. Thanks to the grandchildren—Justin, Jonathon, Megan, Ashlee, Alyssa, and Joey—who bring such delight and new material! Thanks to sister Carol for being such a great reader and editor.

Thanks to the prayer team—Anita, Deb, Mary, KT, Orval, Lucia, Laura, Karen, Charles, Rod, Lil, Wes, Charlene, John, Jeff, and Roxanne—and countless others, for holding us up. Thanks to writing friends like Joan, Jane, Joyce, and the WWCWG, and good friend Jonesy, for your wild enthusiasm.

Thanks to Adult Day Services, Pastor Paul, Peggy, Triniteam, Lisa Wells, and the rest, who encourage and care for the caregivers and for those we love.

Thanks to my dear agent, Lee Hough, supereditor Sandy Vander Zicht, and the great team at Zondervan for continued faith.

And thanks to Kathy and Lindy—chocolate-bearing friends—for standing by and helping share the load.

May God bless you richly, as you have blessed me.

Introduction

Remember Twister? We played the game on a big plastic mat with four rows of colored circles—red, blue, yellow, and green—spreading the mat on the floor like a picnic blanket. We played the game at home, at birthday parties, and at sleepovers. We played the game with siblings, friends, and classmates.

Two, three, or four players in "stockin' feet," the instructions said—stood on circles at the edges of the mat to start. The "referee"—usually the bossiest kid in the bunch—got to spin the cardboard dial (some assembly required) and call the shots. The instructions were simple. Spin the dial. Move hands or feet as instructed. Spin again. Move again.

With the first spin, Bossy gave the order to place the called-out body part on the called-out color. "Right foot red!" *This is nothing*, we thought, laughing to ourselves. *Bring it on!* We put our right foot on one of the red circles on the mat.

Another spin. "Left hand yellow!" *A cinch!* We bent forward to put our left hand on a yellow circle, while keeping our right foot on red. More spinning. "Right hand blue! Left foot green!" We laughed as we became pretzels, our arms and legs twisting over and under one another's. Again and again, spinning and moving, and laughing hysterically, we contorted ourselves. One by one we lost the game as we lost our balance, hitting the mat with elbows or knees. The instructions were simple: touch the mat with any body part but hand or foot and you lose.

The key to winning? Don't fall.

Gamemaker Milton Bradley called it "the game that ties you up in knots." What more could a child want? Playing the Twister game as a kid was fun.

Living the Twister life as a grown-up is not.

But it is a fact: grown-up life has a way of tying us up in knots. We are, at any given moment, either in the middle of a problem, coming out of one, or heading toward one. We all have hassles, headaches, and heartaches—big ones, small ones, and all sizes in-between. And we can feel life spinning out of control; someone else is controlling the dial and calling the shots. Before we know it, we're all twisted up— physically, mentally, emotionally, and spiritually—and it's all we can do to keep from falling on our keister.

We all have those times when we feel our lives have become a game of Twister.

I am one twisted sister. I've been frustrated. I've been afraid. I've freaked out at times. Doubt and discouragement have, at times, dumped me into depression. Oh, the troubles I've seen! Some of my troubles have come from circumstances beyond my control. Some troubles I brought on myself. (Those are the worst, don't you think?)

I saw a sign in a gift shop a while back: "This Is Not the Life I Ordered!" Do you know that feeling? The life I ordered was a life of ease and tranquility, with more than enough of everything I needed. More than enough money, food, and shelter. More than enough fun and frivolity. More than enough time and energy to do all I wanted to do, go everywhere I wanted to go, and be everything I wanted to be. The life I ordered was a life of love and laughter, in which romance lasts forever and the sun is always shining. Such a dream life: happy childhood, fabulous family, and great career.

The life I ordered was a fairy-tale life, a living-happily-ever-after kind of life. Did you order that life too?

I didn't plan on being twisted by troubles. Hangnails. Bad hair days. Traffic jams. Strong-willed children. Orthodontics. Ugly mother-of-the-bride dresses. My mother moving in as the last kid moved out.

Mice in the attic. Squirrels in the chimney. Crow's feet. A dog with a fetish for chicken bones from the garbage. Dog breath.

Losing my shape. Losing my marbles. Forgetting to brush the dog's teeth. My mother getting Alzheimer's.

A leaking roof. A leaking bladder. A leaking mind. Wondering if Alzheimer's is contagious. Humungous vet bills for chicken bone damage and doggy dental work.

I didn't plan on feeling old before my time, or feeling tired all the time. Feeling stretched and twisted and whipped. Out of touch, out of energy, and out of options.

Nope. I didn't plan on any of that. Did you?

What kind of life did you order? How does your reality compare? Have you felt the twisting of life's stresses? Have you ever felt like one more surprise will push you over the edge? Have you ever wanted to scream, "Enough is enough! Stop the game! I quit!"?

So have I.

Where are you today? Have you got trouble right now, or has it just passed? Or do you sense you're heading into it?

You are not alone. Hassles, headaches, and heartaches—we all experience them as we are pretzeled by this Twister game called life.

What's a sister to do?

Laugh, cry, and pray. Beg, wheedle, and cajole. Deny, bargain, and rage. Whine, sob, and surrender. All of the above, yes, but above all this: Don't fall. Stand.

Stand. It's the standing, I'm learning, that gets us through. It's standing on the promises of the one who never changes, never forsakes us, and never fails us. Standing by faith in the one who has everything we need to make it through. The one who understands. The one who loves us through it all.

In the middle of the troubles, the trials, and the twisting, God is there. God cares.

Come along with me now as we look at, laugh at, and maybe even cry together over some of the troubles of life— the hassles, headaches, and heartaches of life's Twister game.

Together, we might find relief. Maybe we can help each other to endure. And maybe, just maybe, together we can find the strength to stand.

Part 1

The Game Begins

"Right foot red!" Bossy calls.
We laugh and step onto a red circle.
"This is nothing," we say. "Bring it on!"

1

Twisted Sister

Whoever said, "Don't sweat the small stuff, and it's all small stuff," never got a good look at my thighs.

I did the other day. It was not a pretty sight. I was in the sporting goods store at the mall. I didn't intend to go in there, but I forgot where I parked my car. (I hate when that happens. It happens a lot. Especially lately.)

There I was, wandering through the sporting goods store, trying to get to an exit. That's not easy. Have you noticed how stores are laid out these days? I've been shopping long enough to remember when you could make a beeline from the front door to the department you wanted and back out again. Now walking through a store is like navigating an obstacle course and requires a degree of agility I don't possess.

Straight aisles are a thing of the past. The art of merchandising is a diabolical plot to trap consumers in the store, expose them to as many displays of goods as possible, and get them so confused and frustrated that they will hand over their wallets gladly, just to be able to escape.

So, trapped as I was, I had little choice but to wander through the displays of camping, skiing, boating, snowshoeing, hiking, biking, treading, kayaking, swimming, lifting, running, scuba diving, fishing, tennis, baseball, racquetball, basketball, football, soccer, lumberjacking, and whaling equipment. Somewhere between the fishing tackle section and the football tackle department, I found myself trapped behind a rack of tiny—*tiny*—swimsuits. There wasn't enough fabric there to cover my left elbow, much less the dimpled tundra of my backside.

Even worse, I was sandwiched between the rack of tiny suits and a huge mirror. These stores have mirrors everywhere. I guess the jock-types who hang out at sporting goods stores don't mind looking at themselves. I try to avoid my reflection, but like those people who slow way down to gawk at a freeway accident, I can't resist sneaking a peek anytime I pass a shiny surface. (Oh admit it! You do it too.)

This wasn't just one full-length mirror but a three-sider. I gaped. I stared. I gawked. The shorts I'd tossed on for this "quick" run to the mall were rumpled and riding up embarrassingly. And there, hanging out like two giant stuffed sausages, were my thighs, glowing under the fluorescents like two gargantuan, pasty-white slugs under a black light. It was obvious why I no longer buy corduroy pants (Aye, there's the rub!) or *any*thing made of spandex.

The tiny swimsuits mocked me from behind while the triple mirror tripled my lumps. Tripled my lard. Tripled my dimples. Ouch. Ouch. Ouch.

Triple mirrors do nothing for a sister's self-esteem.

"Who *are* you?" I whined at the three women in the mirrors. "How did this *happen*? You used to be in great shape. You were fit and flexible, tight and toned in high school!"

We used to dance *in high school*, they reminded me.

Glory Days

Standing there before the jiggling blobs of my current reality, I drifted back to those glory days of youth, when the lower half of my body actually had muscle.

It's true. I used to dance. Modern dance was one of the physical education electives in our high school. I elected it. We modern dancers worshiped at the bare feet of our teacher, Miss Jeanne, who had worshiped and studied at the bare feet of modern-dance-maven Miss Martha Graham, *herself*! Under Miss Jeanne's skilled tutelage we learned how to dance like the wind, soar like the eagle, wave like a field of wheat, and rise like the sun. All within the confines of the gym at North High.

Modern dancers, Miss Jeanne showed us, could isolate their rib cages from the rest of their torsos, elevate any given body part, and stretch in ways that seemed humanly impossible (to say nothing of painful). Modern dancers had steely thighs and elastic hamstrings that allowed them to float across the floor with power and grace.

And six of the modern dancers in our class were chosen to be the horses in the merry-go-round when the senior class put on a production of the musical *Carousel*. Each of us was assigned a position and a color. I was the pink pony.

Upright in pastel leotards and matching tights, we six pranced proudly, each holding in her pony forefeet a length of wide pastel ribbon. The opposite ends of the ribbons were attached to a tall center pole.

The tall pole was a girl named Jane. The least graceful horse in the class, Jane held the ends of the ribbons high as we swifter ponies trotted around her. She raised and lowered the ribbons as we raised and lowered our steely thighs in a graceful canter, moving around and around with us, faster and slower, higher and lower. At times we even reversed direction in a dazzling feat of merry-go-round marvel.

Opening night came. Around and around we pranced. No one noticed that Jane, who'd performed her part flawlessly during rehearsals, had decided not to wear her glasses in front of an audience. (Vanity of vanities!)

Jane, blinded and dizzier by the minute, evidently lost track of whether the pastel blur surrounding her was moving clockwise or counterclockwise. Unable to judge the speed or direction of the herd, Jane did the only thing a pole could do. She stood still.

We ponies cantered on, not noticing until it was too late that the pole was frozen. Soon poor Jane was mummified in pastel ribbons and we horses were falling over each other as we wound ourselves closer and closer to the center. The carousel ground to a halt. So did the play. So did my dancing career.

Reality

Snapping back to the reality of the sports store's three-way mirror, I shuddered to realize how far my body had deteriorated—from the glorious days of fresh lean youthfulness to the flabby nag, sagging like a feed sack of cellulite, staring back at me. The old gray mare just wasn't what she used to be; she looked ready to be put out to pasture. *Neigh.*

I slunk away from the mirror, hoping no other shoppers had seen me there, in triplicate. One of me was bad enough.

Depressed, I wove my way through the rest of the store, avoiding the mirrors and focusing on the merchandise instead. I wondered why they call the stuff "sporting goods." Most of it seemed neither sporting nor good.

Think about it. Who in her right mind binds her stiff-booted feet onto flat fiberglass slats and hurls herself down a frozen mountain, protected only by her fluffy pink jacket and matching fluffy pink headband? Wouldn't a fluffy pink crash helmet be a good idea?

Who in her right mind wedges her oversized bottom into an undersized kayak and paddles alone out into the middle of a lake? Doesn't she know that when the thing capsizes—and it will; it will!—her smaller top half will never be able to counterbalance the centrifugal force created by the larger ballast of her bottom in motion? She'll be trapped there under the water, waiting to drown. Upside down!

Sporting? Good? I think not.

"What's a girl to do?" I asked the handsome mannequin modeling the latest in spandex exercise wear. He had no answer. He may have been a dummy, but he looked good. Everyone, it seemed, was in better shape, thinner, fitter, doing more, going faster, and running farther than I was. I wanted to scream, "Where is the stuff for girls like me?" Girls who are a little long in the tooth. A little short of breath. A little wide in the angle. A little narrow in motivation.

Just then, as if to answer my question, a peppy girl in a store uniform bounced up to me. She was young enough to make me wonder if the child-labor laws were still in effect.

"Can I, like, help you?" I could tell from her tone she thought I was beyond help. I wanted to ask her to escort me to the nearest exit and maybe help me find my car, but I suddenly felt the need to make her think I had *something* on the ball.

"I need to start working out. What do you suggest?" She gave me an appraising once-over and led me down a nearby aisle. She plucked a book called *Walk Yourself Fit* from a rack and handed it to me.

How had she guessed walking was my sport? I had decades—over twenty thousand days so far—of walking practice. I was good at walking. A quick glance at the book's back cover assured me that I could quite literally walk my way to fitness and good health. I didn't need to do anything but walk. No need to change my diet. Walking would automatically, over the course of time, cause my thighs, indeed all of me, to shrink miraculously and painlessly.

Walking I could handle. The price of the book—$9.95—I could also handle. I was ready to head to the huge sign that said CASHIER—they make sure you can find those—when the nice young lady said, "You'll need some walking shoes. They're right over here ..."

A hundred-and-eighty-seven dollars later, I left the store with the book and its accompanying CD of walking music. I had new shoes—a dynamically engineered, air-cushioned, shock-absorbing pair that specialized in walking. (Did they even need me?) I had air-cushioned socks that were guaranteed to absorb the shocks the shoes missed, even if I had trouble absorbing the shock of forking over twelve bucks for a pair of socks. (Socks!)

I had new shorts and a matching shirt that were guaranteed never to shrink, fade, or wrinkle, no matter how much abuse I subjected them to. (Oh, for a body with that kind of guarantee!) And the shorts were friendly; they promised not to pinch me, squish me, or ride up and wedge themselves into uncomfortable places. My new sports bra was positively aerodynamic and designed to hold me firmly with no sagging for five years or fifty thousand miles of bounce, whichever came first.

And with it all, *le pièce de résistance*: new undies that breathed. How could I resist? They *breathed*, for goodness sake! (How had I made it all these years wearing suffocating undies?)

I was set. The cashier pointed me to the exit; I eventually found my car and drove home with the sort of radiance that only a good day's shopping can bring. I glowed all night. I was still glowing the next morning, when, headphones pumping CD motivation into my brain and clad in my new shorts, shirt, bra, shoes, and socks, and with my undies breathing the fresh morning air, I set out to walk myself fit.

Five minutes out, halfway up the first hill, my formerly elastic hamstring twisted itself into a knot the size of my fist. I hobbled back down the hill before the first song ended on the CD, limped into the kitchen, where I sat and sipped a double cafe mocha with extra whipped cream for consolation.

Life is full of twists, isn't it? It's hard sometimes to navigate from one spot to another without getting trapped or hurt or lost. Life doesn't seem to have clear wide aisles that allow us to flow easily from one place to the next. Lots of the things that happen to us are not what we'd call good or sporting.

And sometimes we just plain forget where we left the car, or our minds, or our hearts.

We can get ourselves all twisted up trying to keep it all together physically, mentally, emotionally, and spiritually. Sometimes we're like the merry-go-round horses; around and around we go, faster and faster, high-stepping and showing off for all we're worth. Sometimes we don't notice what's happening until we're all twisted up in the ribbons of living and come to a crashing halt. Sometimes we don't notice the pole standing there nearby, paralyzed and blinded by the chaos we've created with all our whirling around.

When we compare our lives and ourselves to what we see around us—and we so often do that—we end up feeling we're not good enough, fit enough, young enough, smart enough, old enough, thin enough, pretty enough, spiritual enough—what*ever* enough—to be worth loving. Worth anything.

I've struggled with my physical image much of my life. I've often felt awkward, clumsy, or just plain ugly. Sitting there in my kitchen I could hear, in my mind, all the names I'd called myself, and all the names I'd imagined or heard others calling me, over the years.

Thunder Thighs. Whale Woman. Blubber Butt. Flat Chested. Slope Shouldered. Squinty Eyed. Flat Nosed.

What have you heard? How have you felt?

God has another perspective.

As I sat there, with my leg propped on the chair next to me to stretch my twisted muscle, I remembered something from the Bible about my being "fearfully and wonderfully made."

Are you serious, Lord? I asked, gazing down at my cheesy thighs. *This is fearfully and wonderfully made? This body?*

"Yes," I heard him whisper to my heart. "This."

Is it possible? Can it be? "I created your inmost being; I knit you together in your mother's womb. You are fearfully and wonderfully made," he says. Can it be true?

Can God really mean that about me? About you?

Yes. This timeless truth is the beginning of our healing, our deliverance from the worry and doubt that plague us. This is the beginning of new life, of a powerful sense of self, realizing that it is God—Almighty Creator of the Universe God—who created us—you and me—and God who loves us. That this physical body, whatever its size or shape, whatever flaws we think we have, is a work of genius.

If God thinks you're a work of art, who are you to argue?

Fearfully and wonderfully made, dimply thighs and all, I am a masterpiece of his design, beautiful in the eyes of my creator. He's called me by new names. To him, I am Beloved. To him, I am Delightful. To him, I am Wonderful.

And so, dear reader, are you.

For everything God created is good.
—1 Timothy 4:4

* *

Points to Ponder

1. Powerhouse or Powder Puff? Describe your experience as a "student athlete." What do you remember about gym or physical education classes?

2. Have you ever been called a name? What did the experience teach you? Have you forgiven the name-caller? If not, when will you let it go?

3. God loves you and he delights in you, according to Zephaniah 3:17: "The LORD your God is with you, he is mighty to save. He will take great delight in you, he will quiet you with his love, he will rejoice over you with singing." Which truth from this verse is most meaningful to you today?

* *

2

The Ideal Woman

Speaking of dimply thighs, June Cleaver and Carol Brady, perfect TV moms of the 1960s and 1970s respectively, didn't have them. (Cellulite was not invented until the 1980s when Jane Fonda, the mother of aerobics, discovered a dimple on her left quadriceps and launched a multi-billion-dollar industry to combat it. The rest is history.)

June and Carol had more in common than cottage-cheese-free thighs. They had perfect hair, perfect houses, and perfect manners. They never screamed, threw things, slammed doors, or ran crying from a room. They never threatened to strangle, maim, shoot, murder, or otherwise bring physical harm to any other living thing.

June and Carol never snored, got bloated, had a cramp, or threw up. And they most certainly never passed gas. No, those TV moms were perfectly controlled in all aspects of their suburban lives.

What kind of role models were they? What images of impossible perfection are wedged into the psyches of millions of women today, despite our protestations of being liberated from the constraints of those fixed gender roles? Let me just grab my white ruffled apron with the pink polka dots, whip up a batch of made-from-scratch brownies, and tell you what I think.

June and Carol got us all twisted up. Something in our brains, deep down in our psyches, tells us that they are the ideal woman and, if we just follow their lead, we can be the ideal woman too.

Our childhood neighbor, Lucille, tried to be the ideal woman. She wanted to be June Cleaver. Her lawn was perfect. If a dandelion dared creep across the property line from our yard to hers (under cover of darkness, for no dandelion dared trespass in daylight), Lucille was out there at daybreak with her Weed Weasel in hand and a bottle of Dandelion Death holstered to her side.

By the dawn's early light, Lucille could be heard muttering as she weaseled the hapless dandelion from the dirt, "Gotcha, you rotten bugger!" Then, with a maniacal laugh, she drew the spray bottle like a Smith and Wesson, took aim, and cackled, "And don't come back!" as she shot poison into the hole. Bam, bam, bam, bam, bam, bam! She was a dead-eye, Lucille was.

Lucille's children were like her lawn. Clean cut and weed free. And under control. The sound of food fights never emanated from her kitchen windows on summer evenings—not that we could have heard them over our own squabbling. Her children, Roscoe and Rosie (my friends), had better table manners than I did. They had better table manners than Emily Post.

Roscoe and Rosie never sat sulking over cold Brussels sprouts congealing in butter sauce, whining about having to clean their plates. (My older sister eventually tried to force my cold sprouts down my throat. I blame her for my lifelong aversion to those diminutive demon cabbages.)

While we were scarfing down all the Turkish taffy and Twinkies we could finagle, Lucille's children were asking—begging!—for green pepper slices for snacks. They willingly obeyed Lucille's post-Halloween candy rule: one piece a day for seven days, and the rest gets tossed.

Seven days? Halloween candy at our house rarely lasted seven hours. We had the cavities to prove it.

You'd never find a wrapper from an illegal Snickers bar in mid-November stuffed between the box spring and mattress in Roscoe's room. Unlike our mother, Lucille never had to wonder why one side of her child's bed was suddenly higher than the other. (That takes a lot of candy-wrapper stuffing, by the way.)

Lucille was a model of homemaking and mothering perfection, everything in order, and everything—seemingly—under control. Was there a Lucille in your neighborhood? In your house?

Who showed you what being a woman was all about? Maybe you never watched TV moms. Maybe you weren't influenced by a neighborhood Lucille. Maybe all the moms in your neighborhood were normal people. Maybe you got your unrealistic expectations somewhere else. Maybe it was the Bible.

Domestic Divas

Maybe it was that woman in Proverbs 31, that biblical home-management diva who did it all and was admired by all for it. Of course, back in Bible times women had it easy. A bath once a month, no makeup, long hair, two outfits and one pair of shoes make for a pretty uncomplicated grooming routine. A dirt floor to sweep, a couple of cooking pots, a couple of jugs, and a few bowls to wash equal a pretty short housekeeping to-do list.

Shopping and menu planning couldn't have been real hard either: go to the well, pluck a chicken, milk the goat, grind some wheat. Really, where was the challenge?

Imagine the woman of Proverbs 31 transplanted to today's world. Fast forward to the Proverbs 2031 woman.

The Bible says that Mrs. Proverbs 31 was up before dawn. Ms. Proverbs 2031 is up before dawn too so she can do her Pilates and get in a five-mile run before the kids get up. Back home, stretched, flexed, and awake, she showers with exfoliating scrub. She gets dressed, choosing from two dozen potential outfits. Her makeup routine involves a dozen products. Coifed, pressed, made-up, and dressed, she is finally ready to meet the day.

In the kitchen, she finds a cup of hot coffee ready for her; she set the automatic brew timer the night before. She heads into her home office to read her Bible and pray. She does her daily planning—five minutes of focused decision-making during which she identifies her three most important outcomes for the day: be a good and godly wife; be a marvelous mom; be a whiz at business. Then she prays for help, wisdom, strength, and anything else she's going to need.

Half an hour later, the children and her husband are up. Breakfast, schoolwork, gym clothes, lunch money—all are dispatched efficiently. She drives carpool, dispatching hugs and kisses as she drops hubby at the train and the children at school. Back home, she pours a second cup of coffee and heads into her office to work.

Mrs. Proverbs 31, the Bible says, worked "vigorously." Today's woman works vigorously too, at a job she loves. Actually, she created her own business after she invented a better mousetrap. She sells them through her website, which she designed herself after taking some graphic design courses on the internet. Her website and her blog on entrepreneurship for work-at-home moms get thousands of hits a month.

Bible woman "considers a field and buys it; out of her earnings she plants a vineyard" (verse 16). Today's woman also invests in real estate. She bought a starter home before she was married and scored a dandy profit in a strong sellers' market; she bought another house and made a killing on that one too. Thanks to the Federal Reserve dropping interest rates, she recently refinanced the mortgage on the family home and put the extra monthly income into mutual funds pegged to the S&P 500. She reinvests the dividends for retirement.

She keeps a little "fun money" on the side for the odd stock investment, and like her counterpart from the olden days, her "trading is profitable" (verse 18). Incredibly profitable, actually, thanks to the high-tech boom and her foresight in selling high and moving to cash just before the dot-com bubble burst.

Mrs. Proverbs 31 burns the midnight oil; her "lamp does not go out at night" (verse 18). Today's gal is up late too, taking a little "me" time to scrapbook the family's vacation photos and then organize her recipe collection. (Did I mention she's a gourmet cook?)

Mrs. Proverbs 31, the Bible says, "selects wool and flax and works with eager hands" (verse 13). Her modern-day equivalent does the same thing; she works with eager hands at the keyboard, finding great bargains online, selecting washable, no-iron, indestructible clothes for the kids and designer duds for herself and her hubby at deep discounts.

Just as Bible gal was "clothed in fine linen and purple" (verse 22), today's gal dresses well too in timeless separates.

She's read enough books and watched enough experts on TV to know what to wear, what not to wear, how to dress for less, and how to dress for success. She knows how to dress for her age, her body type, her lifestyle, and her budget. Color her gorgeous!

Bible woman is a generous woman, who "opens her arms to the poor and extends her hands to the needy" (verse 20). Today's woman donates a portion of all she earns to the needy too. She serves holiday meals at the local homeless shelter and visits the folks at the nursing home several times a year. She volunteers in the church nursery and leads a Bible study. She participates in several Run for a Good Cause events each year. And the whole Proverbs 2031 family volunteers in the summer to build houses with Habitat for Humanity.

Bible woman has no worries about her household when the snow comes, "for all of them are clothed in scarlet" (verse 21). Our gal is likewise confident. She is on her driveway as the first flakes fall, yelling, "Let the winter winds howl! Thanks to the Do-It-Yourself Network and Home Depot, my whole house is clothed in insulation: R-44 in the attic and R-19 everywhere else. I've caulked every crack and every cranny. I'm weather-stripped. I'm weather-proofed. Old Man Winter, give us your best shot!"

Whew! The ideal woman is a hard act to follow, isn't she? She does it all and does it all well. Do you ever feel the pressure to be like her? I know I do.

The Booby Hatch

Here is the other side of the story. Back in our old neighborhood, Lucille seemed to have it all together, but Lucille was a mess. She had what we used to call a nervous breakdown and ended up in what we used to call the booby hatch. (Roscoe Senior took the kids and moved to Scottsdale to live with his mother, who was, in his opinion, the only perfect woman in the world to begin with, but that's another story.) Control is what Lucille wanted. In trying to get it, she lost everything.

Control is what June Cleaver and Carol Brady seemed to have, but life isn't a television script. When June and Carol took off the aprons and left the television studios, they went home to their own kitchens, their own families, and their own problems. They went home to real life.

Real life is hard. Stuff happens in real life. Real life for the Proverbs 31 woman was hard, of course. Imagine life without medicine, microwaves, or makeup! Life was hard for Lucille, and life is hard for all of us too.

But of all the women mentioned, the one in the Bible knew best. She figured out the truth about control. The truth is this: God is in control. We are not.

Because she knows *that* truth and builds her life on it, she is "clothed with strength and dignity" (verse 25). She pays close attention to everything that goes on in her home. She can laugh at days to come for she is well-prepared—that is, trusting God for the strength to deal with whatever the future may bring. Others listen and appreciate her advice— probably even her teen-aged daughters—because "she speaks with wisdom, and faithful instruction is on her tongue" (verse 26).

How does she do it? Because she is a woman who fears the Lord, and out of that reverent awe, she draws her strength, wisdom, and balance. This is the secret godly women know—that the ideal life is not a life that's lived perfectly but a life that's lived reverently. It's not about *being* all things to all people at all times. It's not about *doing* it all or *having* it all. What matters is *giving* your all—all of your heart, mind, body, and soul—to God first and, having done that most important thing, trusting him to show you what comes next.

What do others think of this woman of noble character? She's "worth far more than rubies" (verse 10). (Today, she'd be worth her weight in T-bills.) Her husband has full confidence in her. He trusts her, for she does him good and not harm.

Her husband and children count their blessings, having such a woman in their lives. In fact, Mr. Proverbs 31 tells his wife, "There are many virtuous and capable women in the world, but you surpass them all!" (verse 29 NLT).

Or, as Mr. Proverbs 2031 might say, "Baby, you're the greatest!"

What was true back then is still true today: "Charm is deceptive, and beauty is fleeting; but a woman who fears the LORD is to be praised" (verse 30). The woman who "fears the LORD" knows a beauty far more lasting than mere physical charm, a powerful beauty that emanates from a humble heart, from a spirit bowed in reverence before Almighty God. She longs to live her life in his presence, guided by his hand, as she loves and serves others in his name.

The ideal woman's life—a real life with all its joy and sorrow—is a God-centered life. Then and now, God's ideal woman lives life well, in the center of his grace.

> You should clothe yourselves instead
> with the beauty that comes from within,
> the unfading beauty of a gentle and quiet spirit,
> which is so precious to God.
> **—1 Peter 3:4 (NLT)**

❋❋❋❋❋❋❋❋❋❋❋❋❋❋❋❋❋❋❋❋❋❋❋❋❋❋❋❋❋❋❋❋❋❋❋❋❋❋

Points to Ponder

1. What does it mean to be a real woman? Who showed you an example you wanted to follow? Who showed you what not to be?

2. Who is following your example of womanhood? What are you showing them?

3. How much of a control freak are you? In what area is it hardest to give up control? What do you imagine will happen if you let go? Pray about letting go.

❋❋❋❋❋❋❋❋❋❋❋❋❋❋❋❋❋❋❋❋❋❋❋❋❋❋❋❋❋❋❋❋❋❋❋❋❋❋

3

High-Maintenance Woman

Flashing red and blue lights in the rearview mirror are quite the little attention getter. The nice police officer approached my car and asked kindly to see my driver's license. He asked me if I knew how fast I was going. Oh, I did. I was speeding. I admitted it.

"But," I explained, "I have a good reason, though it doesn't excuse my breaking the law, of course, but you see, officer— sir—I have to get to the nail salon at the minimall before they close because I have a big fancy party to go to tonight and well, I broke a nail ..."

A very, very, *very* expensive nail, as it turned out.

I've had my nails done professionally for years. I was a nail-biter in childhood and all that biting must have discouraged the little buggers from growing. Think about it: would you stick your head out if it was going to get bitten off every time?

The only time I've had good nails was during pregnancy. Three times in my life, I've had nice natural nails. A total of twenty-seven months I had moon-shaped moons and hard white tips on nails that glistened with robust health as they grew and grew and grew. I'd have had a dozen more babies just for the great nails, but I discovered right away that, after delivery, you have to take the babies home and raise them. And as much as I love my children, having babies just for the nails isn't that great a bargain in the long run. In the long run, it's much cheaper to go to a professional.

Getting artificial nails may seem silly to you. You've probably got naturally gorgeous, pregnancy-pretty nails. You've never known the humiliation of stubby raggedy nails, or the shame of sensing others' better-than-thou haughtiness at your lack of good grooming.

You've probably never had to wear Stop Biting Forever— the thick, red nail-biter repellant polish that my mother put on my nails. It was supposed to taste awful.

I learned to love its piquant flavor, with its cinnamony aftertaste.

And you've probably never lived with the terror of knowing what happens to girls who bite their nails. Growing up, we heard—on the playground, so we knew it was true—that if you bite your nails, little slivers of fingernail can accidentally fall down your throat and end up sticking to your appendix. Later, when you least expect it, such as on your wedding day, your appendix decides to burst open right in the middle of the ceremony, in front of God and everybody, including your future mother-in-law, who has suspected all along that you might not be good enough for her son.

The emergency room X-rays show that—sure enough, just like your mother warned you—your poor appendix is filled to bursting with bits of fingernails. Your husband-who-almost-was looks at you with pity mixed with better-than-thou haughtiness. Your almost-mother-in-law leads her son from the room, whispering assurance that there are other girls in the world for him—better, non-nail-biting girls.

You're relieved, actually, because you'd been dreading the Picture of the Rings that the wedding photographer was going to be taking later, the picture where you lay your left hand on top of your new husband's perfect left hand to get a picture of your gorgeous new wedding bands. You dreaded it because you'd been trying to grow your nails out since you got engaged a year ago. But the little buggers refused to grow ("We're not coming out! You'll just bite our heads off!"), despite your daily application of triple coats of nail-biting repellent. And now, to make matters worse, you realize you're addicted to Stop Biting Forever. It's that irresistible cinnamon aftertaste; it's like a childhood comfort food to you now.

Tips of the Iceberg

I envy the girls to whom God has granted the gift of healthy, natural, *free* fingernails. I envy the girls to whom God has granted the gift of natural beauty that requires no intervention. Bless them! I am not among them. And my fake nails are just the tip—or tips, rather—of the iceberg, for I am, I confess, a high-maintenance woman. And getting more so by the year.

It used to be so simple to be presentable. It used to be I could wash my face in the morning with warm water and a little Noxzema, pat dry, and then glow with freshness all day long. My former splash-and-go skin-care routine is now a twelve step program. (Is there a meeting somewhere for women like me? "My name is Mary and I am addicted to microdermabrasion. Oh, and also Stop Biting Forever …")

Wet, cleanse, exfoliate, microdermabrade, alpha-hydroxify, condition, and tone. Apply eye-bag shrinking miracle formula that promises, "Visible Results in Thirty Days!"

(It's been thirty years, but who's counting?) Apply eye-area brightener to eye area that grows duller by the day.

Moisturize with secret daytime, age-defying, wrinkle-erasing formula, fortified with vitamins C and E, aloe vera, lecithin, glycerin, collagen, essential amino acids, and the kitchen sink. Moisturize again with a second daytime formula, this one superenriched with isopropyl this and poly-wolly-doodle that. Oh, and it is SPF 30. (In case you haven't heard, the UV ray is *not* your friend. Stay away!)

Next apply special invisible concealer to disguise spots, blots, and lines. Apply foundation, a little lipstick, and, on top of it all, a dusting of fine translucent powder that acts, for the moment, like a filter over the camera lens. Admire how I look ten years younger. Allow a moment to blink, which clears the fine translucent powder dust from my contact lenses. Look closer and hope that nobody else ever gets close enough to see what I'm seeing. Turn out the light and leave the bathroom. Avoid mirrors for the rest of the day.

Each evening the twelve steps are reversed. At least they are on those evenings when I have the energy to do anything other than flop into bed. (The appalling decrease in energy and the astounding increase in the number of programs I simply *must* TiVo for bedtime viewing seem to be related, but I haven't got the energy to figure out how.)

So if I can summon the energy, I remove my makeup. Remove the eyelid-lifting miracle cream. (I hear a soft thud as those eyelids fall.) Remove what's left of the incredible eye-bag shrinker. Remove from all the spots, dents, and creases the once invisible concealer, which at this point in the day has turned to congealer. Remove the blush that gave me that youthful glow until it glopped into my crow's feet. Remove the lipstick that looked oh-so-kissable for a second; now I have a map of the Red River and its tributaries above my mouth.

Remove it all and then cleanse with the *nighttime* cleanser, followed with the *nighttime* age-defying, secret moisturizing formula. On top of all that, slather on three other moisturizing products designed specifically for *nighttime* use to (1) incredibly shrink my eye bags while I sleep, (2) amazingly fade my skin spots while I sleep, and (3) condition my lips so they'll be extra-oh-so-kissable while I sleep. (Why I need kissable lips while I sleep I can't imagine.)

Top it all off with a thick layer of the vitamin-enriched, anti-oxidant-laden, aloe-enhanced, nighttime moisturizing cream with green tea extracts. A cream that makes alligator-rough skin softer than a baby's bottom in the commercials. A cream that smells vaguely like Noxzema. Hmm.

In a rare and lucid moment, I wondered why I needed two products that seemed to do the same thing by day and by night. I wondered if I could have saved some money on, say, eye-bag shrinker. Do eye bags undergo some profound physiological change under the effect of daylight, some change that makes my morning bag shrinker less effective under cover of darkness? I can't take the chance, so I buy both products.

I also wondered if I could buy eye-bag shrinker in larger quantities—a fifty-five gallon drum maybe—and use it on my saddlebags. These are the questions that keep me up at night. Which increases the size of the eye bags. It's a vicious circle, isn't it? Or maybe a conspiracy powered by the cosmetics industry.

Your makeup routine tells a lot about you, according to an article I read recently. For instance, if your makeup bag contains only lip gloss and light blush, you are probably afraid of color. Ha! If you need only gloss and blush, you are obviously young and have nothing to fear—from color or anything else. Enjoy it while you've got it, baby!

On the other hand, the writer said, if the bag contains hot red lipstick and glittery eye shadow, you are a risk taker. Well, that's a no-brainer. Women with hot red lips and glittery eyes take risks—like being on the street after dark wearing fishnet stockings with a vinyl miniskirt. Risking arrest. Not a look I would risk trying.

Use makeup to enhance your natural beauty instead of masking it, according to the expert. That advice is obviously not meant for those of us who need a paint-sprayer and a fifty-five gallon drum of concealer. Or eye-bag shrinker.

"Pinched cheeks" are in style too. Great news! I can do pinched. Pinched as in "I just slammed my finger in the door!" Pinched as in "I'm in labor and I want to kill somebody!" Pinched as in "I should not have eaten three helpings of sauerkraut last night." Like I said, pinched I can do.

But if it's true—and I know it is because I read it in a magazine—that "that healthy glow" is in fashion, then I give up. I am now, and will forever be, hopelessly out of fashion. If I ever glow again, it will be because I fell into a nuclear reactor.

Higher Maintenance

What, oh what, is the point? So much time, energy, and money spent on making the outside of me look presentable, working to prevent—or at least delay—the onslaught of aging. Is it desperation? Is it fear that drives me? Is it denial of the fact that this body is "wasting away" like the Bible says?

What is the point of all this self-preservation? Do I want to be so well preserved that centuries from now, archaeologists will dig me up and say, "All these years and her skin looks so good!"? I've seen King Tut. No amount of pomegranate moisturizer, oil of asp, or extract of Nile would have helped him. Given time, we all kind of look alike, don't we?

So why bother with the maintenance routine? Is it desire to fit in with the rest of society, which seems to focus only on outward appearance? I've bought into more of the culture's message than I like to admit—this quest for, if not beauty, at least some semblance of physical attractiveness.

But how can I justify spending so much time and energy, and cold hard cash, on myself and how I look when there are so many needs out there and so much suffering?

What's the bottom line? Is it a sin to take care of the skin you're in? Or is it okay for a God-fearing woman to exfoliate? Since this physical body of mine is the temple of the Holy Spirit, then I have an obligation to maintain the building, don't I? I want to take care of myself. I want to feel good. All of that temple-tending honors my creator. Call it good stewardship, or sound natural-resource management. Consider it wise personal ecology.

But where do I draw the line? I imagine myself speeding through life, driving as fast as I can in the wrong direction—away from God and toward self. I see the lights flashing red and blue in my rearview mirror. God pulls me over. "Stop and think," he says. "What is your life when a broken fingernail becomes your chief concern, when your looks matter more to you than your character, when life revolves around the next shopping trip or the latest exercise routine, when your biggest worry is what you're going to wear tomorrow?"

To paraphrase the Bible, what does it profit a woman to primp and preen and polish her physical self and lose her own soul—her real self? This body—my physical self, and yours too—is indeed wasting away. From the moment we are born, we begin the process of dying. The message is clear: life on earth is short! And between birth and death, God has more important things for us to do than to obsess about our image.

God has a better life in mind for me—a less self-absorbed, more generous life. He has so many other—better—things in which to invest my time, energy, and money than in my own high maintenance. Things with value—for this life and the next. Things that allow me to be a blessing to others.

Comforting and praying for others. Holding babies. Playing with grandchildren. Laughing with friends. Loving my family.

I don't need God to pull me over and write me a ticket. I get the message. Slow down. Pay attention to what matters. Live.

> Set your minds on things above,
> not on earthly things.
> —Colossians 3:2

* *

Points to Ponder

1. How has your personal maintenance routine changed over the years? What's easier now? What's more difficult?

2. What about your body makes you self-conscious? What about your body do you love? Decide today to accept the body you are in, just as it is. Ask God to help you love who you are, just as you are.

3. Think of one "better" thing you'd like to spend time on. (More time with friends? With family? Volunteering? Praying?) Take time this week to bring blessing to the lives of others.

* *

4

So Much Advice

My daughter, home visiting from college for the weekend, left a note on the cupboard on Saturday morning. "If you're looking for more fiber and protein in your breakfast, try this new cereal." She'd brought her own. I grabbed the unfamiliar box next to the note and read the ingredients. Wood chips. Seaweed. Lawn clippings. Well, not exactly, but close, and just one more example of a supposedly good food that seemed to me to be neither good nor food.

I reached in the box, grabbed a nugget, and sniffed. A faint scent of newly mown hay. I laid it on my tongue, where it began to melt, releasing a slightly kelpy taste. I chewed it up. It had the texture of sawdust.

Hummph! I hummphed, as I poured myself a fourth cup of coffee and popped another Pop-Tart into the toaster.

It's hard to know what's good for me these days.

My husband, Terry, lifted his coffee cup yesterday at breakfast and asked the most FAQ of late. "Is this good for us or bad for us?"

"Today I think it's good for us," I said. I'd read something about coffee drinkers having less chance of getting some dread disease. "But that could change any minute."

When one study concludes that coffee has benefits, another study says coffee does the body more harm than good. Tea is a far better choice, say some. But what kind of tea? "All natural" is the way to go, they say. But I wonder, is there unnatural tea? A synthetic tea? Polytea, like polyester? Isn't everything that grows in nature "natural," by definition?

Green tea seems to be all the rage. So does that mean we say so long to oolong? What about black? I was shocked to discover they all come from the same place: tea plants. Who knew!

If I make the switch to tea, how should it be prepared? There is a whole culture centered on "proper" tea preparation. Should I follow the Eastern traditions? And if so, should it be Japanese, Chinese, or Tibetan? And must I meditate, mull, and muse while I sip? (I'm not sure I have the attention span for that.)

Or will the Western tea style be better for me? If so, will it be Western as in oh-so-veddy-proper English with pinkies up and china cup? "Lemon? Milk? Another scone, my dear?" (I'm not sure I have the doilies for that.)

Or will it be Western as in Rocky Mountain High Colorado, with a mug of Wild Blue Yonder herbal tea steeped in mountain spring water that's been heated gently over an open fire? "Seeds? Nuts? Granola scone anyone?" (I'm not sure I have the Birkenstocks for that.)

Too many choices. Too much temptation to spend a fortune on proper tea paraphernalia. I'm too old a dog to learn a new tea service. So I'll take my chances with my coffee, thank you veddy much.

Back at the breakfast table, Terry poked at the fried eggs on his plate. "How about these?"

"Eggs are good, I think. The whites, at least, because they don't have any fat. Or is it cholesterol? Or maybe it's the yolks that are good because they have iron. Or maybe because they're yellow."

"Butter's yellow. Does that mean it's good?" He sounded so hopeful.

"I think it's saturated," I said.

"With what?"

"Fat. Or maybe cholesterol. Or both. Or maybe food coloring. That makes you hyper."

"Then I could use a little food coloring this morning," he said.

"I know some kind of fat is bad," I said, "but which one? Is it saturated? Is it mono, poly, or trans fat that we're supposed to watch out for?"

"Mono, Poly, and Trans? Weren't they folksingers back in the sixties?"

"That was Peter, Paul, and Mary."

Terry sighed. "I wonder what they ate for breakfast ..."

To Eat or Not to Eat

To eat or not to eat. That is the question these days. What's good for us one week will kill us the next.

Just when I thought it was safe to hit McDonald's again—protein is good, they told me—I heard that red meat is out. Its muscle-building benefits are outweighed by its artery-clogging propensity. I think. But then I just heard again the other day—on television, so it must be true—that beef is "what's for dinner." But is hamburger okay, or is sirloin steak the only acceptable beef? Do corn-fed cattle produce high-carb beef? Just curious.

Chicken is better, some say. But not the skin or the visible fat. And not the dark meat. And never fried, braised, dipped, battered, or sautéed, and certainly not in a bucket of any kind. Maybe we'd be better off chucking the whole chicken and eating the feathers instead.

Fish is best of all, I've heard. "Fish is brain food," Grandma used to say, slurping down her third helping of lutefisk. [Lutefisk: *LOO-da-fisk. n.* from Norwegian *lut* (stinky) + *fisk* (glop). A lye-soaked, gelatinous hunk of cod slurped during holidays by Scandihoovians and other palate-challenged peoples of the world, despite the fact that nobody in the last two generations has actually admitted to liking the stuff. See also: Fish Head Casserole, Whale Blubber Soup, and Salmon Eye Surprise, all of which have about as much appetite appeal as the week-old take-out sushi you forgot in the trunk of the car.]

"Fish is brain food," Granny used to say. "Headache," I say, as Dr. Seuss and I try to figure out which fish is best.

> *Which, oh which? Which fish is best?*
> *Ocean born or deep-lake fresh?*
> *Bred on farms or swimming free?*
> *Which, oh which, is best for me?*
> *From a can or "previously frozen"?*
> *Hard to know when best I've chosen.*
> *Mahi, flounder, salmon, trout,*
> *it's hard to figure fish stuff out.*
> *Fish for brains just can't be beaten,*
> *but lutefisk? Best left uneaten.*

The nutritional key with fish—the "brain food"—is in the fishy fatty acids, I'm told. But is it omega-3s I need? Are omega-6s twice as good? And I thought fat was the enemy. Is fish fat my friend?

It's all so confusing.

"Don't worry about the fat! Sugar is the enemy," some diet gurus say. This week. A friend's father proved to be ahead of the times when he swore off sugar years ago. He switched to saccharine instead. He's now nearly ninety. I guess he hasn't heard that saccharine will kill you.

The idea that sugar and other simple carbs are bad makes me sad. It's the end of an era. Wonder Bread—the bread that fed a generation; the bread you could form into little balls to flick at your brother—*thwap!*—when your mom's back was turned; the bread that built "Strong Bodies Twelve Ways!"—is on the endangered species list. So is everything Little Debbie's little face made us crave. (So innocent! So wholesome! Who could resist her?) Twinkies and Ding-Dongs are *snackae non gratae*. The Ho-Ho is a big, fat no-no!

Banished forever—for our own good, they say—are all the highly processed, overly sugared, and fondly remembered foods. What happened to Sugar Corn Pops and Sugar Frosted Flakes? They're still out there, but they are in stealth mode, marketed without the *sugar* in the product name. Oh, for the good ol' days and the good ol' cereals that made no pretense of being good for me!

Oh, for the good ol' days when we sang, with the Dough-boy, "Nothin' says lovin' like somethin' from the oven." It was my theme song. Is there a better cure for what ails us than the smell of freshly baked chocolate-chip cookies? Is there any trouble that can't be helped by a warm slice of homemade apple pie and a big scoop of vanilla ice cream? Mary Poppins had it right; there is nothing so difficult in life that "a spoon-ful of sugar" won't help.

But those days are gone. Sugar, fat, and flavor—the main ingredients in comfort—are forbidden. It's all about "good" grains these days. Good bread is whole grain, high fiber, and "all natural." (Natural? Again, I ask, is there a synthetic bread? Oh yeah. Wonder.) Are seven grains enough? Are twelve grains too many? And which grains should they be? Oat, wheat, rye, corn, or barley? That's only five. What are the others? Sawdust? Seaweed? Lawn clippings? You do the math.

Two dollars and eighty-nine cents a loaf, or three dollars and twenty-nine cents a loaf? All lined up next to the two-for-a-buck generic Wonder-like breads. It's hard to choose. I might have to get a second job to support my "good" bread habit.

So Much Advice, So Little Wisdom

So much advice! Overwhelming at times, isn't it? I catch myself going glassy-eyed, in danger of an information overdose from reading labels, studying the new science of nutrition, and listening to the latest advice. Advice from the diet doctors, who conspire to keep us confused as they take turns making fortunes off our confusion. Advice from the friend who lost forty pounds in forty days eating only lard and grapes. So much advice can leave us in a state of analysis paralysis. We can't do everything, so we opt to do nothing.

But there is a far greater danger to our health than junk food. Bombarded with so much advice and so many choices about what we stuff into our mouths, we start to think that's all that matters. We forget to think about what goes into our hearts—our spiritual hearts.

For that, God's "eating advice" is simple. Jesus summed it up: "People do not live by bread alone, but by every word that comes from the mouth of God" (Matthew 4:4 NLT). The word of God is the soul's sustenance. That's always been true, and always will be. He who created us knows what's best for us. He designed us to benefit—spiritually, yes, but also physically, mentally, and emotionally—from his every word.

It doesn't benefit us at all to feast on the food of this world if we are starving to death spiritually. What is spiritual starvation? Refusing the lifebread offered to us. Jesus gives us this picture: "Yes, I am the bread of life! Your ancestors ate manna in the wilderness, but they all died. Anyone who eats the bread from heaven, however, will never die. I am the living bread that came down from heaven. Anyone who eats this bread will live forever; and this bread, which I will offer so the world may live, is my flesh ... I live because of the living Father who sent me; in the same way, anyone who feeds on me will live because of me" (John 6:48–51, 57 NLT).

Why would I choose to eat the food of this world alone when Jesus offers me a feast—the very Bread of Life—for this world and for eternity? The choice is mine. And yours.

I want to pay attention to what I'm eating on this earth, eating as healthy and sensible a diet as I can stomach (I'm a temple, after all), but I want to be even more purposeful about my spiritual diet.

Jesus taught us to ask each day for God's provision, "our daily bread." We need that physical sustenance, of course, but we need the daily Bread of Life as well. Daily, I want to dine at God's banquet table, the table overflowing with his love and truth. Daily, I want to feast on his every word.

Tomorrow morning, I'll be feasting on my daily Bread, God's good word, taking in his wisdom and peace along with my breakfast of egg-white omelet and a slice of multigrain, preservative-free, high-fiber bread (lawn-clipping free, according to the label) topped with a no-sugar-added, fruit-only spread. I'll pop a multivitamin, just in case my actual food is missing something vital. And I'll wash it all down with my coffee.

Coffee? It's good for me, at least for this week. I think. Bread of Heaven? Good for me forever. No doubt about it.

> Blessed are those who hunger
> and thirst for righteousness,
> for they will be filled.
> —Matthew 5:6

❋❋❋❋❋❋❋❋❋❋❋❋❋❋❋❋❋❋❋❋❋❋❋❋❋❋❋❋❋❋❋❋❋❋❋❋❋❋

Points to Ponder

1. What was your favorite childhood treat? What made it so wonderful? When did you have it last? Was it still wonderful? (If so, stock up and enjoy it!)

2. What are your comfort foods? What memories are associated with them? What role do they play in your life today?

3. What does it mean to you to "hunger and thirst for righteousness"? In what ways are you eating right, spiritually? In what way would you like to change your spiritual diet?

❋❋❋❋❋❋❋❋❋❋❋❋❋❋❋❋❋❋❋❋❋❋❋❋❋❋❋❋❋❋❋❋❋❋❋❋❋❋

5

Wake-up Call

The alarm blasts my 5:00 a.m. wake-up call. I roll out of bed, stumble to the bathroom, stumble back to the bedroom, and roll out my exercise mat. I hit the play button on my CD player to start the soothing instrumental accompaniment to my morning stretch routine.

Back in my peppier days, I exercised with Jane Fonda and her friends to videos of her heart-pounding, high-impact aerobics classes. I used to holler along with Jane, "Woo hoo!" and "Oh yeah, baby! I feel the burn!"

Now "oof!" is my first word of the day as I lay down on the mat. Arms reaching over head as my legs extend, I feel my body elongating. I'm trying to reclaim the half inch I've shrunk in the last decade. I elongate as long as I can; I relax and shrink back to normal.

Then, arms out to my sides, I bend my knees toward my chest. *Snap, crackle, pop,* say my knees. *Gurgle* is my stomach's answer. I groan as I lower my bent knees together to my left, then my right. *Creak,* says my hip. *Crack,* says my back. "Crazy," says my mind. My body used to be much quieter when I moved.

I return to where I started, flat on my back on the mat. I reach for my canvas strap, loop it around my right foot, and extend my right leg up into the air. The hamstring stretch. Hamstring torture is more apt. I repeat with the left leg. Torture times two. Once upon a time, back in my pony-prancing days, I could bend over and put my nose to my knees. Now those were hamstrings!

I roll over to my stomach and raise my body into a flattened "plank," my upper body supported by my forearms and elbows and my lower half by my toes. Being a plank uses every muscle I have. Being a plank requires stamina. I count to twelve before I collapse. That's a big improvement. I started at zero. Six months ago. That's two seconds per month. I'm a planking whiz!

After planking, I push my palms into the mat as I raise my hindquarters up, legs straight. I look just like the dog when she does her morning stretch; hence the term for this posture: downward-facing dog. Woof. My stomach growls again. I growl back.

I stand upright, then raise my arms overhead for the final stretch. As I stretch heavenward, I'm praising the Lord, thanking him for a new day. Thanking him that I was able to get up off the mat. I look back at my bed with longing. I'm pooped.

I stumble back into the bathroom and look in the mirror. Saggy, Baggy, Droopy, Lardy, Lumpy, Flabby, and Pooped. Snow White's friends have come to live in my body. But I know that I—we all—will persist and hopefully tomorrow, but definitely the day after that, we'll stretch again.

We Know. We Know!

I'll stretch. I'll walk. I'll lift. I'll drink water. I'll watch what I eat, most of the time. I will try to do, some days more, some days less, the healthy things that countless experts tell me I should do, all drummed into my brain by an endless stream of advice-givers and self-improvement gurus. Repeated again and again, on television, radio, and internet. In magazines, books, and newspapers.

Physical maintenance is an industry that advertises incessantly. We know what's good for us. The daily "high five" of dark green leafies, cruciferous crunchies, and citrus juicies combined with plenty of H_2O, lean proteins, and whole grain fibers make for a clean running system. Enough rest to rebuild our bodies, combined with enough movement to tire us out so we can sleep better, will keep us going strong. We know the drill. *We know!*

When I speak for women's wellness events, I ask for a show of hands: "Is there a woman here who does *not* know she is supposed to drink more water? Is there a woman here who does *not* know she is supposed to get regular exercise? Is there a woman here who does *not* know she is supposed to eat right?"

Nobody ever raises a hand, because we all *know* what to do. We just don't always *do* what we know we should do, do we?

What we lack is not information. What we lack is incentive. Sometimes we need a wake-up call.

Our wake-up call came with the cardiac treadmill stress test the doctor ordered after my husband complained of fatigue and occasional shortness of breath. We blamed his symptoms on being middle-aged and out of shape. Terry went in on a Wednesday afternoon at three o'clock for the test; we planned to go out for Mexican food when the test was over.

When the nurse brought Terry back into the waiting area in a wheelchair, I sensed we wouldn't be heading for El

Burrito Grande. "We're admitting him," the nurse said. Terry had an angiogram the next day, which revealed nearly complete blockage in all three main coronary arteries. Quintuple bypass surgery the following week saved his life.

We woke up. Exercise, eating better, regular checkups, more rest, less stress — all those things we *knew* we needed suddenly became priorities. God had given us a medical wake-up call. We heard him loud and clear.

Has God given you a wake-up call? Test results outside the norm. Worries about nagging symptoms. Suspicious signs. A genetic predisposition to a disease or syndrome. Hearing the word *biopsy* or *malignant*. The death of someone younger than you are, a death that might have been postponed had they just been paying attention.

These are wake-up calls from God. What will it take for you to hear? What will it take for you to take better care of yourself, to pay closer attention to your physical maintenance? Since we're going to be living on this earth for a while, it makes sense to do what we can to maintain our bodies, to be as healthy, sharp, strong, and nimble as we can, for as long as we can. Taking care of the "temple" is important. (How I empathize with the woman who said, "My body's a temple, but the congregation has outgrown the building.")

Paul writes, "God's temple is sacred, and you are that temple" (1 Corinthians 3:17) and "Do you not know that your body is a temple of the Holy Spirit, who is in you, whom you have received from God? You are not your own; you were bought at a price. Therefore honor God with your body" (1 Corinthians 6:19–20).

As important as physical health is, it isn't the only concern in this life. There must be a balance — not just of carbs, fats, and protein but of body, mind, and soul. There must be a balance—not just stretching and strengthening physical muscles but stretching and strengthening the muscles of faith as well.

Taking care of my physical self is a means to an end. I am supposed to take care of this "temple," this temporary housing, so that I can get physical concerns—all that self-concern—out of the way.

Let me say that again: Taking proper care of my physical self gets my concern for my physical self *out of the way*, freeing me emotionally, mentally, physically, and spiritually to focus on what *really* matters. Taking care of my physical self means that I will be energized, strengthened, and equipped to physically do what God put me on this earth to do: to follow the Holy Spirit's leading to love and serve God by loving and serving others.

But medical issues aren't just a call to take better care of your body. They are also a call to godliness. They are God's reminder that we are mortal human beings who will one day stand before him to account for our time here on this earth. Personal trainers, dieticians, and aerobics instructors can provide valuable guidance in physical maintenance, but God is the one who calls the shots.

Calling the Shots

Think about it. As the psalmist says, "I lie down and sleep; I wake again, because the LORD sustains me" (Psalm 3:5). We wake again, surviving the night, because the Lord sustains us. We draw our next breath, and the next, because God says we can. We don't wake up unless he allows it. That's the bottom line for us fragile and finite human beings, isn't it? We are not in charge. And it scares us, so we deny our fragility and our mortality by focusing on youth, physical beauty, and strength. And our culture encourages that obsession.

Jesus asks in Mark 8:36 (NLT), "What do you benefit if you gain the whole world but lose your own soul?" I ask myself, how do I benefit if I can plank for an hour without a quiver, lift a ton without a wince, run for miles without a cramp, but I forget about my eternal soul in the process? How do I benefit if I have the tautest abs, the lowest cholesterol, and the healthiest colon on the planet if I lose my way spiritually, for eternity?

Consider the apostle Paul's advice to his protégé Timothy. "Train yourself to be godly. For physical training is of some value, but godliness has value for all things, holding promise for both the present life and the life to come" (1 Timothy 4:7–8).

What is this "training in godliness"? Training to run the marathon of God's calling on us. Training to develop the stamina we need to stay the course of life, long after youth and physical attributes have faded. Training to breathe in the Holy Spirit daily, so that we can run without fainting.

Training so we will be able to rightly exercise our will when priorities and desires collide. Paul describes life's marathon like this: "I press on to take hold of that for which Christ Jesus took hold of me.... Forgetting what is behind and straining toward what is ahead, I press on toward the goal to win the prize for which God has called me heavenward" (Philippians 3:12–14).

Spiritual maintenance, like physical maintenance, is about stamina. It's about pressing on, strengthening the muscles of faith and trust, so that, in the time of testing, we can hold on.

And the time to start building your spiritual strength is now. Today. Paul writes that another reason for right living is that we "know how late it is; time is running out. Wake up, for the coming of our salvation is nearer now than when we first believed" (Romans 13:11 NLT).

Paul told Timothy that training in godliness holds "promise ... for the present life." That promise is, I think, a promise of blessing that comes when we focus daily on God's will, on his daily call to love and serve him. The "promise of godliness" in this present life is the contentment and peace that come from knowing—having tested the truth and trusting in it—that God has everything under control.

But the promise of godliness is not just for this life but also for the "life to come." Salvation. Heaven. Eternity in the presence of complete love. Eternity with God.

We were "bought at a price," God's Word tells us. Jesus "bought" us at the cross. Jesus bought our frailty and our infirmities. Jesus bought our disease-ridden hearts, our cancer-wasted bodies. At the cross, beaten, bruised, and broken, in his own frail and finite, pain-wasted humanity, Jesus surrendered to death, "once for all." And in doing so, he bought us life.

Life everlasting, yes. But also "this present life." Here. Now. Today.

A dear friend called the other day. "I have breast cancer," she said. She's forty-two. I hung up the phone and cried. And I prayed. Everything falls into place in a moment like that. The earthly clock is running for each of us.

Nothing in this life matters as much as how we connect with God and others. Today. "Encourage one another daily, as long as it is called Today.... Today, if you hear his voice, do not harden your hearts" (Hebrews 3:13, 15).

God's call is clear: we don't have forever to do what we are here on earth to do. We have today. This moment. It's time to wake up.

> Morning by morning he wakens me
> and opens my understanding to his will.
> The Sovereign Lord has spoken to me,
> and I have listened.
> —Isaiah 50:4–5 NLT

✳✳✳

Points to Ponder

1. List five things you know you "should" be doing to maintain your health. How consistent are you? Set one health-improvement goal for the coming week. How will you achieve your goal? (Have you been postponing a call to the doctor? Call today.)

2. Describe a physical or medical wake-up call you or someone else you know received. How did you or they respond? Do you know anyone who woke up too late? What were the consequences?

3. What are the signs of vibrant spiritual health? How is your spiritual health these days? What can you do to improve it? Set one spiritual-health goal for the coming week. Pray for wisdom. Ask the Holy Spirit to help you achieve your goal.

✳✳✳

6

My Eyelashes Hurt

My preschooler came to me one long-ago day and hugged me. I hugged her right back. "My arm hurts," she said.

I looked at the spot she pointed to. "I don't see anything there," I said.

"I meant it's my leg," she said. I examined the proffered limb.

"Hmm. I don't see any owies there either."

She blinked her big blues at me and said, "My eyelashes hurt." I got the message. She wanted to be held, comforted. She wanted Mommy to kiss away all the boo-boos, all the owies, and all the problems of her little life.

So I did.

Ah, life was so much simpler back then.

Today the kids call to talk about marriage issues, financial issues, parenting issues, and their doubts and fears. Today the news is full of war and rumors of war, disasters, diseases, and distress. Wouldn't it be wonderful if we could just kiss away all the bad stuff of life?

Wouldn't it be wonderful if someone could do that for us? We hurt. We worry. We grieve. We struggle. Where is the rocking chair for us? Where are the strong arms? Where is the lap, always available for our comfort and consolation? Where is the reassurance of, "There, there now … Everything is going to be just fine"?

It's been many years since those preschooler days, but lately I feel like I'm back at it. Having my ninety-something mother living with us and needing care has brought back that bone-tired feeling that comes after you've taken care of everyone else all day long and just want someone, anyone, to take the burden for a little while. When the babies were tiny, I often wished someone would rock *me* for a change and sing me a lullaby. When the children were older, I longed for someone else to take care of daily duties once in a while and give me a little break. (How did my grandmothers do it, one with ten children and the other with fourteen, and no washer and dryer? No dishwasher. No McDonald's. Talk about a Twister game! How *did* they do it?)

I've had a lot on my mind lately, and a lot on my plate. Life's convoluted. Life's contorted. Life's out of control. Somebody—not me—is spinning the dial and calling the shots. Where is the predictability that preserves my sanity? Where is the order and organization that offer me comfort in my chaos?

"Only in the arms of Jesus," I've heard. The advice to "give it to the Lord" or "let go and let God" feels trite today. I know I need to "give it to the Lord," and I do. But then, so often, I take it back again—usually because the Lord isn't fixing things fast enough to suit me. Isn't that ironic—taking it back because he isn't fixing it fast enough, when I gave it to him in the first place because I couldn't do anything to fix it? Silly me.

Lord, my eyelashes hurt …

Midnight Musings

Journal: July 5, 2:33 a.m. "I try to sleep but my mind won't rest. I'm awake in the middle of the night, sitting at the kitchen table in the semidarkness. 'We have lost our ability to see in the dark,' the science expert said on TV last night. The show was about light and our human desire for it. Later, I watched the fireworks over Boston harbor on television. In past years, we've gone to the local park, with the rest of the city, to watch the live fireworks. But not this year. Why not? No energy. No desire. No drive for anything lately, except home and hoping to find some semblance of order in this chaos. Besides, Mother doesn't do well outside in the dark, and crowds stress her out."

We recently cancelled an out-of-town business trip because nobody was available to take care of my mother. I don't like thinking that my mother is cramping my style, but, frankly, my life has been turned upside down with her living here. She is losing her ability to handle the ADLs—activities of daily living. I do all the cooking, cleaning, and laundry. I make sure she is wearing clean clothes, and I fix her hair for her. I make sure she gets her eye drops and her hearing aid. I take her to her doctor and beauty appointments. I dole out her vitamins and make sure her coffee is hot. I fix her ice cream for her bedtime snack.

But there is more to it. Her "executive reasoning" is going, going, gone; she can't remember the steps in a process or the rationale for wise decision-making. She can't really be left alone, so we got her an emergency Help Button to wear around her neck, just in case we have to leave her for a short time.

Such was the case late one fateful Friday afternoon. My car had been in for repair and Terry and I had drive to the car repair shop to pick it up. We hung the Help Button around Mother's neck. "We'll be back in about a half hour," I said. "Don't push this unless you've fallen and can't get up!"

I was heading back home in my car—no more than fifteen minutes after we left—and the Help Button people called my cell phone. "We've had an alarm at your house and didn't get any answer when we called to check it out. The paramedics are on the way."

Heart in throat, I floored it and beat the ambulance to the house. When I rushed in, there was Mother sitting exactly where I'd left her, watching *Oprah*. After making sure she was okay, I asked, "So why did you push the button?"

"What button?" she asked. I held the necklace out from her chest. "This button! You pushed it and now the ambulance is on the way!"

She stared down at the button. "Oh, is *that* what that is? I didn't know what it was, so I pushed it." The paramedics arrived a few minutes later and came in to make sure she was okay. Then the sheriff's department stopped in to verify that there was no emergency. "Nice to meet you," she said. She acted like they'd just stopped by to say hello.

Later we laughed about it; Terry teased her about her "run-in with the cops." "Well," she said, "it's been a long time since I had so many handsome men in my room." At least we know now that the Help Button works.

Her short-term memory gone, Mother lives in the moment, and while she is 100 percent there in the moment, it is still only the moment. Not yesterday. Not this morning. Not fifteen minutes ago. Just the moment.

Her eyesight is going—she has glaucoma—but yesterday she sat in the sun reading *Tom Sawyer*, which she said she is enjoying now more than when she read it as a child. And I ask myself, what is more important in life—the ability to organize your sock drawer, or the ability to enjoy a great book? Even if you are enjoying the same book over and over and over again. (She says that one advantage of losing her memory is that she doesn't need an extensive library.)

Helping Mother with her ADLs is why we are here. We are providing her "assisted living." It's the right thing to do, as Paul wrote: "But if a widow has children or grandchildren, these should learn first of all to put their religion into practice by caring for their own family and so repaying their parents and grandparents, for this is pleasing to God" (1 Timothy 5:4).

Taking care of my mother is the right thing to do. It is a joy and a blessing. And it is difficult and exhausting. It is the best of times. It is the worst of times. All at the same time.

Lord, I know that taking care of my mother is pleasing to you. But my eyelashes hurt . . .

God and Uncle Bill

My first memory of praying for others involves my mother's brother, Uncle Bill. I was eleven years old when Uncle Bill, a construction worker, had a cerebral hemorrhage while working the jack hammer on a site in downtown Minneapolis. He was rushed to the hospital, where he clung to life. I heard the worried talk among the grown-ups. I was worried too, so I went to pray in my room.

I had this secret, after all, this amazing God thing happening, something the adults in the family didn't have. I knew Jesus. Personally. I'd met him, and what a Friend I had in Jesus! He was the best Friend I could have ever wanted, for just such a time as this—the first true crisis I'd encountered since Jesus had come to live in my heart. I prayed to God, my Friend, that my uncle would not die.

But Uncle Bill died the next day.

What was I to think of God? That he hadn't heard me? Not a chance; he was the omnipotent God. He heard everything. I knew he'd heard and I knew he could have done something to keep Uncle Bill alive, to heal that cerebral whatever-it-was. But God chose not to.

What was I to think of God? I couldn't have articulated it then, but I got the feeling that God might be like a lot of other grown-ups I knew. He listened; he seemed to care; but he couldn't be counted on. Like the earthly father I knew *(Oh, Daddy, you missed so much!)*, who was a real nice guy but, because of his drinking problem, couldn't be depended on to bring home the paycheck, much less the miracle!

God was capricious, blown by every wind, one moment a lover of my soul, and the next, a coolly distant judge. One minute hearing me, loving me, and holding me, the next minute far away and busy. Too busy to save Uncle Bill. Too busy to care whether I hurt. Too busy with his agenda, what with the world needing to be saved and all. God was too busy for me.

I've grown up since then. People are capricious; God is not. People may be blown by every wind; God changes not. People may be too busy for us; God never is. God is the constant, consistent, and all-powerful Friend. Powerful enough to rescue. Wise enough to know that rescue is not the best answer every time. Sometimes the struggle is the answer.

But we want deliverance, not struggle. What we want is the answer *we* want, not something that God decides is better for us. What we want is to be at ease, in comfort, at peace, and delivered out of our problems. We just want our troubles to go away.

We want Uncle Bill to live.

In His Company

Our eyelashes hurt. So do our backs, our bodies, and our brains. We work and we worry. We grieve and we struggle through hassles, headaches, and heartaches. Where is the cosmic rocking chair for us? Where are the strong arms to hold us? Where is the lap for our comfort and consolation? Where is the hushed reassurance of, "There, there now ... Everything is going to be just fine"?

Where they have always been—in the presence of God Almighty. God's power is not limited by the circumstances of today. It's available to us, just as it's always been. We just need to open our eyes, ears, minds, and hearts to it. As Paul put it, "I pray also that the eyes of your heart may be enlightened in order that you may know ... his incomparably great power for us who believe. That power is like the working of his mighty strength, which he exerted in Christ when he raised him from the dead" (Ephesians 1:18–20).

It is that incomparably great resurrection power that is available to us today. And God is in control. God has a plan. God has the power to bring it all to his conclusion. And in the process, he offers us comfort, courage, power, and peace—even in the darkest and most difficult times—if we will just come to him.

Andrew Murray, in *Waiting on God*, expressed his desire to make patient waiting on God a "continuous habit of the soul." A. W. Tozer, another faith giant, expressed a desire to be "much in his [God's] company."

How do we tap into the incredible peace and incomparable power of God? By developing that continuous soul habit of being "much in his company." Day by day, moment by moment, having an awareness of his presence. Entering into his presence (what a privilege!) and waiting, still and expectant, before him. Finding light for our darkness. Finding help for our hurts.

Much in his company, we find peace. "Don't worry about anything; instead, pray about everything. Tell God what you need, and thank him for all he has done. Then you will experience God's peace, which exceeds anything we can understand. His peace will guard your hearts and minds as you live in Christ Jesus" (Philippians 4:6–7 NLT).

A child comes to a parent, craving company, expecting to find comfort and peace, understanding and help. The child comes, expecting to feel safe in the parent's arms.

And just like that—with that same childlike expectation—we may come into the presence of God, where we are never disappointed. There, in his company, God keeps his promises: "Peace I leave with you; my peace I give you. I do not give to you as the world gives. Do not let your hearts be troubled and do not be afraid" (John 14:27).

Into his company, in trusting anticipation, we come.

And without faith it is impossible to please God,
because anyone who comes to him
must believe that he exists
and that he rewards those who earnestly seek him.
—Hebrews 11:6

****

Points to Ponder

1. Describe your biggest childhood "owie." Was it a physical, emotional, or spiritual hurt? Who comforted you as a child? To whom do you offer comfort today?

2. Describe your first encounter with the power of prayer. What did you pray for? What was the answer? When has God's answer been no? What was your response to that? What do you think today?

3. Where does it hurt? What is the source of your pain? What does God say about it? What comfort do you find in his company?

****

Part 2

All Twisted Up

"Right foot red! Left foot yellow!
"Right hand blue! Left hand green!"
Again and again, spinning and moving,
we contort ourselves, adjusting
as the game ties us up in knots.
One by one we lose the game
as we lose our balance.
The key to winning? Don't fall.

7

All Twisted Up

Picture this caricature: a man stares, his bloodshot eyeballs bulging from his eye sockets as a dozen lit cigarettes dangle from his mouth. The top of his head enveloped in a cloud of smoke, he stares at his crashed computer; he looks like he is, literally, about to "blow his stack."

This is the picture I show audiences when I speak on the subject of stress.

In one recent session, I put the slide up and a woman in the back row yelled out, "That looks just like my husband!" The woman next to her yelled, "That's right! It *does*!" The first woman then hollered, "He's my biggest stress-maker!" and her friend added, "That's right! He *is*!"

The woman's husband is obviously a carrier. He probably doesn't think he has any stress at all, but he certainly seems to give it to everyone around him—and their friends.

Do you live with a stress carrier? What's stressing you out today? What's that, you say? You have no stress? Quick! Have someone take your pulse. Stress is part of being alive. What we call stress is the body's reaction to anything and every-thing, good or bad, that happens to us.

Good stress—and yes, some of it is good—results in posi-
tives like motivation, goal-achievement, and a resulting sense
of well-being. Good stress is what keeps us moving forward
toward what we want in life. Good stress is, well, good and
necessary. Think of it as "positive energy." Think of it as a
blessing.

But we're not talking about good stress in this chapter.
We're talking about bad stress, the kind of stress that brings
on discouragement, fatigue, and even illness. The kind of
stress that can make you feel like you are about to blow *your*
stack. The kind of stress that, left unaddressed, can kill you.

We're talking about the kind of stress that sends us into
distress, the kind of stress that makes you want to reach out
and smack the next mealy-mouthed Pollyanna who tries to
tell you, "Stressed is just 'desserts' spelled backward!" You
want to give them their "just desserts" on the spot. That kind
of stress.

What are the sources of stress—the stress-makers—in
your life? Imagine a score card on which you can give yourself stress points. Following is a highly unscientific look at the
major sources of stress in life. How does your life add up?

1. Children

How many do you have under your roof? Give yourself fifty
stress points for each child under the age of one. Quadruple
that if you have two children under the age of one and they
are not twins. Yikes!

Give yourself twenty points for each child under five.
Twenty more points for each month you've been trying to
potty-train without success. Fifty more if you and your untrained tyke are now having adultlike conversations about

the whole issue. My friend asked her little guy why he didn't want to wear "big boy pants" like the other boys in nursery school, and he insisted, "I'm a *baby*! I wear *diapers*!" He's in an Ivy League college now, so there's hope. And that same friend, as an untrained tyke herself long ago, had informed her mother, "When I'm weady to twain, I'll twain." (What goes around, comes around.)

Give yourself thirty stress points for each teenager. A hundred points for each teenager with a driver's license. Add one point for each dollar your car insurance has increased as a result. A hundred points for each time the teen driver returns the car with (a) no gas, (b) mysterious dings and dents he or she insists were there before, or (c) a headlight dangling from wires and he or she insists, "I have *no* idea how it got that way!" (It can happen. Honest.)

Fifty points for each child over twenty-two who has (a) never left or (b) left before but "boomeranged" back home. (If your child is living at home and is over thirty, give the kid a hand for finagling such a great deal from parents who should know better. Take a thousand stress points for yourself, and then give yourself a swift kick.)

2. Pets

How much poop do you scoop in a week? Take a stress point for every load you scoop off the street, scrape off the carpet, lift out of the litter box, or shovel out of the barn.

Take fifty points if you have to clean a bird cage. Add twenty five points if the bird is a constant squawker. I bought two parakeets—Tilly and Wink—when my dear old mother moved in with us a few years ago. I remembered how much she loved birds when I was a kid. We always had a parakeet in our apartment, and I grew up thinking that parakeets were sweet quiet pets. Now I realize that was because we had only one bird at a time.

These two buzzards chattered constantly. As soon as the cage was uncovered in the morning, the squawking started. Tilly and Wink paid no attention to the humans in the house; they chattered and squawked to each other all day long.

After a few weeks of this, my mother—you'll recall I bought the birds for her benefit—said, "If those were *my* birds, they'd be dead by now!"

The birds disappeared one summer afternoon, under a cloud of mystery. I'd set their cage (more a birdie condo, really) out on the deck to give them an opportunity to chatter and squawk with the birds of the forest. It also bought me a few hours of peace and quiet in the house.

Mother was on the deck, sweeping away the leaves that had fallen in the previous day's rainstorm. Izzy, the fox terrorist, napped on the deck all afternoon, moving from one warm spot to another as the sun crossed the sky.

Late that afternoon, when I went to retrieve the birds, the drop-down cage door was open. Tilly and Wink had flown the coop.

I questioned the most likely suspect. "Mother, the birds are gone! Any idea how the cage door fell open?"

"Well, don't look at *me!*" Mother said, getting a little huffy. "The dog probably bumped the cage and the door fell open."

"Oh sure, blame poor Izzy," I said.

"Well," Mother said, gathering herself up to deliver her closing argument, "Izzy never liked those birds."

These are the facts of the case: The cage door had been slightly askew earlier. The dog did like to nose around the cage. Mother had been sweeping near the cage and her eyesight isn't so good anymore. Dog or mother … we'll never know. I console myself with the hope that the birds found their way to Florida somehow. Case closed.

Give yourself fifty stress points for each squawking bird in your life. Give yourself a hundred points if you have a squawking mother too.

3. Family

Speaking of mothers, family can be a tremendous source of stress. Give yourself ten stress points for each family member whose calls you don't answer when their number shows up on caller ID. Take fifty points for each time they've shown up at your door, uninvited, in the last month. They knock and before you can run and hide, they've let themselves in. "You didn't answer my call, so I thought I'd better stop by and make sure you are okay."

You stammer, "But what … where   ? How did you get in here?"

"Good thing I had that extra key made when you asked me to come over and take care of the birds for you, huh?" You make a mental note to change the locks.

Add two hundred stress points for every relative of yours who loves the "permavisit." These are the people who use your home, situated as it is in a lovely part of the world, as their vacation destination every year. They show up from the cold north in the winter, or from the hot south in the summer, to visit. But like permafrost, they won't leave.

A month later, your hints fall on deaf ears: "We want to take a few days to redecorate the guest room before you come back," you say. They insist your guest room is just perfect and even more wonderful since they did some rearranging for you. Peeking in, you realize they've added a leopard-print slipcover to your great-aunt's vintage chaise, and matching leopard lampshades to "perk up" the room. They also picked up some paint and, while you were out seeing your therapist, surprised you with new wall color. Too bad their favorite color—chartreuse—is not yours.

So you drop stronger hints. "We have to go out of town for a few days and don't want to impose on you to take care of the house." What you really mean is, *If you people won't leave, we'll have to, but we're afraid you'll steal us blind while we're gone.* They insist, "It's no imposition at all. You go and have a great time; we'll hold down the fort for you!"

You can't stand to confess that you lied about having to go on a trip, so you end up taking a spur of the moment vacation, paying incredibly high peak-season rates at the local resort. You're seething the whole time, realizing what your relatives would be forced to pay if they didn't permavisit for free at your house.

When you return home, you discover—"Surprise!"—they've done a reverse extreme home makeover for you. Your formerly lovely home resembles the "before" pictures.

You finally say flat out, "We're out of food, out of money, out of patience, and out of toilet paper! Get out!" The next morning, they leave. They leave in a huff, but you don't care. You sigh and collapse on the couch.

That evening—you're still collapsed on the couch—the doorbell rings. Before you can run and hide, your in-laws have let themselves in. "You didn't answer our calls, so we thought we'd better just fly down and make sure you are okay. Anyway, Dad has three weeks of vacation he had to use or lose. We'll just take our things into the guest room."

You murmur incoherently, give yourself a thousand stress points and kudos for not killing anybody. Not that you'd be able to muster that much energy.

4. OPP (Other People's Problems)

Award yourself the stress points indicated below for these problems among the people in your life:

- Five hundred points if someone had a baby and needed your help adjusting to motherhood. Double the points if your help was needed in the middle of the night. Triple the points if the baby lives at your house.
- Five hundred points if someone moved from one place to another and needed your help packing and moving. Add another fifty points for each flight of stairs involved. Add a hundred for each couch, mattress, major appliance, and piece of furniture made of MDF (particle board) you helped wrestle from one place to another. Another five hundred points if you've helped these same people move more than once in the last year. (If you needed hernia repair surgery because of them, I can't help you.)
- Five hundred points if someone joined a recovery program — AA, NA, GA, OA, and anything else anonymous — and felt the need to share every detail of every step of their recovery with you. Add a hundred points for every time you've been tempted to overindulge as you listened.
- Five hundred points if someone separated or divorced and felt the need to share every detail of the breakup with you. Add a hundred stress points if hearing their story has made you question your own relationship choices.

- Five hundred points if someone had surgery and felt the need to share every gory gooey detail with you. Add a hundred points if you've had to actually look at the scar, the implant, or the reconstruction. Add another hundred if you have one to match.

Other People's Problems, particularly the recurring ones, can be overwhelming. Sometimes we're tempted to try to fix the problems. Sometimes we stop listening because we can't bear to share any more of the pain. Sometimes we blame ourselves for not doing more, not seeing the problem before it's too late, for not trying harder to help.

Count a hundred stress points for every regret you have that you didn't listen more compassionately, when you had the chance, to a loved one who was sick, in trouble, or in need. Ask God to help you listen with new ears. Ask him to give you wisdom to know who, what, where, when, and how you can best help the people you care about. Ask him to set you free from the guilt you carry because you did too little too late in a situation in which you had no control anyway.

People, people, people! "The world would be a great place if it weren't for the people," according to one wag. Another says, "Everyone is normal until you get to know them." Our involvement with others can result in a gazillion little hassles, headaches, and heartaches. A gazillion ways to twist us into knots. A gazillion reasons to worry, worry, worry. And for what?

Jesus asks, "Can all your worries add a single moment to your life?" Of course not! "And if worry can't accomplish a little thing like that, what's the use of worrying over bigger things?"(Luke 12:25–26 NLT).

What issue concerning family or friends is on your mind and heart today? Are you worried? Are you weary? Take the situation to the Lord in prayer. He cares. He cares.

> In the day of my trouble I will call to you,
> for you will answer me.
> —Psalm 86:7

* *

Points to Ponder

1. Was Ben Franklin right that "fish and houseguests smell after three days"? Who is or would be your fishiest houseguest? What kind of houseguest are you?

2. Do you know any stress carriers? What impact does such a person have on others? What advice would you give to someone who lives with a stress carrier?

3. Think about the family or friends issue that worries you most today. What is the worst possible outcome you can imagine? What is the best thing that could happen? Commit to praying about this issue daily for the next week. See what the Lord can do!

* *

8

Let's Get Personal

It's not always other people and their problems that cause us stress. Sometimes the biggest stress-maker is in the mirror. What about your stuff?

"What stuff?" you ask. Open that closet. Look in that drawer. Check the garage, the basement, and the attic.

"Ohhh ... *that* stuff."

5. Stuff

How many gas-powered items are in your garage or driveway? They are worth thirty stress points each. Another thirty points if you did *not* buy the maintenance agreement and have to manage repairs yourself. Fifty points if the thing breaks down the week after you decided not to renew the maintenance agreement that you bought and never used anyway.

Add fifty stress points for every item of this type you no longer use but still have in your possession. News flash: The dead lawn mower is not a lawn sculpture. It is junk! And so is the rusty 1956 Chevy behind the fence. It's junk no matter how many times you've heard or said, "But she's a *classic* and I'm gonna to fix 'er up someday!"

What's that you say? You don't keep junk? All the junk belongs to the others in the house because *you* keep only *important* stuff? Well, good for you. I used to say that too. But before you make so bold a boast, consider carefully whether, hidden in the dark recesses of your residence, you might find any of the following.

(1) A pile of photographs that will "someday" be in albums, or better yet, in memory scrapbooks. (My imaginary scrapbooks are gorgeous! I wish you could see them. I wish anybody could see them.) Give yourself fifty stress points for each pile or box of "one of these days I'm gonna scrapbook these" pictures and souvenirs.

Add fifty stress points if you have forgotten the names of some of the people in the pictures. Add a hundred stress points if the people you can't identify are your own children.

Here's an idea for all you one-of-these-days scrapbookers. If you have yet to make that memory scrapbook chronicling your baby's life, and the baby is now old enough to have a baby of her own, do this: Tie a pretty bow around the box of pictures and baby memorabilia from your baby's life. Present it to your now grown-up baby as a gift. Tell her to make her own scrapbook. (You can thank me later.)

(2) Bridesmaid dresses, no matter how many times the bride assured you that, unlike every other bride, she chose a dress for you that could easily be worn for other occasions. News flash number two: Bridesmaid dresses are ugly enough the first time around. Hear this: you will *never* wear the dress again! Even if it would miraculously be in style. Which it won't. Even if it would fit. Which it won't. The same principle applies to prom dresses and cheerleading outfits. Give it up!

One exception: your wedding gown doesn't count as junk, unless you've had the dress longer than you had the husband.

(3) A television, radio, VCR, boom box, camera, or piece of computer-related equipment from the last century that doesn't work because (a) you can't find the detachable power cord, (b) the batteries it needs aren't sold in your country anymore, or (c) when you called the repair guy, he said, "You have a *what*?" and started laughing so hard you hung up on him. Count fifty stress points for each of these dead items, and add another fifty points for every year they've been gathering dust. Or mold.

Speaking of mold, add an extra hundred stress points if, when you go to toss the old camera, you find a moldy roll of film in there from your son's second birthday and your son is now twenty-three. (Yes, it can happen.)

If, when you found the old camera and saw the roll of film, you had even a fleeting thought of developing the pictures and adding them to your imaginary one-of-these-days scrapbook, don't give yourself any stress points. Simply go to the nearest wall and bang your head against it repeatedly. Perhaps some sense will return.

Stuff takes time, space, and energy in our lives. Too much stuff and too little time, space, or energy is a recipe for stress. And the more complex our stuff gets, the more stress we accumulate.

How many computers do you own? Add fifty points for each. Add a hundred points each for any electronic items smaller than a bread box. (If you are old enough to have owned a bread box in your adult life and are also expected to be computer savvy, add five hundred stress points. It's that "old dog, new tricks" kind of stress. I feel your pain.)

How many telephones, land or cell, do you have? Thirty points each. Add a hundred stress points if you ever—*ever*—talk on your cell phone while you are driving. Make it five hundred if you and your car are not equipped for hands-free communication. Give everyone *else* on the road a *thousand* stress points whenever you talk while driving.

How many televisions do you own? How many hours do you watch per week? Add twenty points per hour. Did you think watching TV was a destressing activity? Ha! If you have cable or satellite service, you know that having a hundred channels to choose from means saying, "There's nothing good on television" a hundred more times a week. And if your system has recording capabilities—TiVo, DVR, PVR—you have at least double the frustration. "There's nothing good on TV and now I have to record it."

It's stressful to own all that stuff, isn't it? What about the stress of keeping it all managed, arranged, and organized? That brings us to our next stress category.

6. PIPs (Projects in Process)

How many home improvement PIPs do you have going in your home right now? Every PIP is worth between one hundred and ten thousand stress points. You be the judge based on the amount of drywall involved, the number of contractors involved, the amount of money involved, and the amount of time that has elapsed from the day the project was *supposed* to be finished until now. Add them all up, including:

1. Things to install. For example, a wall of bookshelves you bought ten years ago to hold toys and books in your child's bedroom. But the child grew up—shelf-

deprived—and has moved out of the house. A thousand stress points for all the guilt and regrets, which are only partly assuaged by your plans to use the shelves as you transform the empty room, someday real soon, into your new scrapbooking room.

2. Anything that needs to be put somewhere other than where it is right now, and it's been where it is for so long because you couldn't decide where it should be instead. When you finally move the thing, are there dents in the carpeting that you can't brush back to life? Or when you take it down from the wall, do you see unfaded paint on the wall behind where it was hanging and say, "Oh, *that's* what color this room used to be!"? That kind of procrastination is worth at least a thousand stress points.

3. A thousand points for every sheet of unfinished or un-installed drywall anywhere in the house, including the basement and the garage. Drywall that will be used as soon as the Do-It-Yourself Network reruns that great program you watched, "How to Drywall Like a Pro." The show inspired you to get started; you just can't remember how to get finished. Ditto the ceramic or porcelain tile, grout, grout sealer, or tiling tools stashed in any corner of a basement, bathroom, or kitchen, waiting for the DIY rerun of "How to Tile Like a Pro."

   Likewise painting project supplies, anywhere you left them because you ran out of the paint you needed to finish the project and you just haven't made it back to the home supply store. Add a thousand points if, when you finally go, you discover that the paint you need was discontinued five years before.

A word of caution about PIPs involving electricity: electrical wires that are visible from fixtures, outlets, or switches require professional intervention, no matter how many times you've heard, or said, "It's just a few wires. As long as they're not touching, there's no danger." Call the pros before you have to call the fire department.

So far we've covered all the stress caused by other people and the stuff in our lives. It's time to get personal. Real personal.

7. Your Money

How many hours do you work a week? Count the total hours you work at home and away from home. Count the hours of commuting and running errands. Count the hours you spend in traffic and in the drive-through. Count ten stress points per hour for the hours you get paid for; count twenty stress points for each hour you work for nothing. (You stay-at-home parents can thank me later, after the kids are grown and you finally catch up on your sleep.)

Do you carry a pager or cell phone for your job? Any little gizmo required to be on your person is worth another thousand stress points. (Add a thousand more if you've ever been paged or called while taking a bathroom break. Add another thousand if you answered the call while still in the bathroom.)

Add another hundred stress points for each time in a day you think:

1. *They don't pay me enough to keep doing this!* (Add a hundred points for each month you've worked since your last raise.)

2. *How many more seconds until quitting time?* (Add a hundred points for every hour of "required" overtime you worked this month.)

3. *How did such a moron get to be my boss?* (Add a hundred points if you ask that question and you're self-employed.)

Since we're talking about work and money, how many credit cards do you have? Count a point for every dollar in debt you carry. Add a hundred points for every time you were late making a payment in the last year. Add ten points for every dollar you've paid in late fees. Add another thousand stress points to your stress score if you always check caller ID to avoid answering collection calls.

How many months has it been since your last "real" vacation? You know the kind—so far away you can't get a cell signal, and you don't bring your laptop with you. No phone, no work, no hassles. Count ten points for each month since you truly "got away."

Now let's get really personal.

8. YOB (Your Own Body)

How many pounds have you gained or lost in the last year? Every pound, up and down and up and down, counts for ten stress points. Add fifty points for every new diet you've started in the last year. Fifty more for every new diet you've quit.

How many health concerns do you have? How many secret worries about disease? Is there an inherited tendency in your family? Add a hundred stress points for each area that occupies your thoughts in quiet moments.

Add another hundred points for every visit you've paid to a doctor, sick or well, in the past year. Sick or well, it's stressful to have someone squashing parts that resist squashing and probing places nobody ought to be probing. Add a thousand points for each labor, delivery, MRI, CT scan, anything ending in -oscopy or surgery you've endured. ("Routine" surgery is what other people have.) Add a thousand for each time any part of you has been prepped, scoped, tested, biopsied, injected, stitched, scraped, or sent to a lab for further examination. A thousand points for each day, or each hour maybe, that you waited for the lab results.

You get another thousand stress points for a ride in an ambulance and a thousand more if a medical professional shouted "Clear!" or "STAT!" in your vicinity.

Oh, how life can stress us out! I don't know about you, but I could use a hug right now. How many days since you had a real hug? One woman counted one point for every day of the seven years since her husband passed away. "He gave me my last real hug," she said. A point a day adds up when you're lonely. A lover's hug is wonderful, yes, but is that the only kind of hug that counts?

Don't let this day end without hugging someone. Hug your friends, hug your enemies. Hug anyone you can legally hug. Hug yourself if nobody else is around. Hands-on hugs are great but you can also hug somebody by phone or via email or in a note. Send the note, make the call. Hug creatively and often!

Let God hug you. Here, paraphrased, are some assurances from God's Word. Take these things to heart: "I have loved you with an everlasting love. Draw near to me and I will draw near to you. Never will I leave you. Never will I forsake you. This is love—not that you loved me but that I loved you first."

Let God cherish you. Let him wrap you in the warm embrace of his unchanging love. You are not alone.

How stressed are you right now, thinking about all your stress? Stress can leave you, well, stressed! All twisted up in knots.

What, if anything, can be done about it? Plenty! Help is on the way!

> Have mercy on me,
> O Lord, for I call to you all day long.
> Bring joy to your servant, for to you,
> O Lord, I lift up my soul.
> —Psalm 86:3–4

Points to Ponder

1. How does your life add up? Identify the number-one stressor for you in each area:

   children   money
   pets   work
   family   physical health
   other people   emotional health
   stuff   spiritual health
   home

2. For each of the above, pray and then write out your ideal vision. For example, what would an uncluttered home look like? What would ideal physical health look like for you?

3. Choose one area. Begin to brainstorm possible actions you can take to reduce the stress and move toward the ideal. (Don't judge your ideas, just record them.) Begin praying about your ideas. Commit to taking one small step toward the ideal. Watch what God can do!

9

Today the Sweatshirts

I took the professional closet organizer's television advice and took everything—"Everything!" she'd said—out of my closet. The bed was soon piled high with debris.

Shoes, purses, belts, hangers, lingerie, socks, sandals, high heels, nylons, knee highs, sweatsocks, shorts, sports bras, workout clothes, sweatpants, sweaters, dress shirts, T-shirts, sweatshirts, skirts, slacks, jeans, belts, purses, scarves, pajamas, and running shoes. And one dress.

Into my six foot wide closet, I'd crammed sixty feet worth of stuff.

You can tell a lot about a woman from the stuff in her closet. According to my debris pile, here are the facts of my life. I was once the "Property of the Athletic Department" of a major university. I've attended Harvard, Yale, and Princeton, if owning the sweatshirt means anything. (It doesn't.)

It's obvious, judging from their pristine condition, I've never actually worked out in most of my "workout wear." It's equally obvious from the fading and sagging—not just me but my garments as well—that I have spent major portions of my life in baggy sweatpants and oversized T-shirts. And the T-shirts tell my life story:

I was "Born to Shop." I was "Born to Garden." I was "Born to Be Wild." Other T-shirts have announced to the world at times that I had a "Baby On Board," then became "She Who Is to Be Obeyed," and the reason: "Because I'm the Mommy—That's Why!"

More recently I've been "The Queen of Everything," as well as "The Only One Who REALLY Knows What's Going On."

I've also been, on occasion, "With Stupid."

One reason my closet is so full is that I have no dresser. Yes, I am a woman to be pitied! I have no dresser! No bureau. No armoire. No highboy. Hard to imagine, isn't it, that a middle-class American woman in the new millennium would have no drawers for her drawers?

My closet is full of plastic bins instead. One bin holds lingerie, though I use the term *lingerie* loosely. I don't shop at Victoria's Secret. I usually buy my undies at Target. Why pay all that money for something nobody's going to see? Ever.

Another bin holds my socks. I love my socks. They are all white, athletic-type socks. Some of my socks are short—so short that they slide down and disappear into my sneakers. At least they did until I discovered those little socks with the dingle balls on the heels. Genius!

Some of my socks are ankle length. I bought a bunch of those the summer I lost weight and my "cankles" went away. (Who was the brilliant woman who came up with *cankle* to describe the legs that flow from calf to ankle without disruption? She must have been nine months pregnant at the time.)

But most of my socks are calf-length, white crew socks. Sometimes I pull them up as high as I can just to torment my daughters, who can't imagine a worse fashion *faux pas* than wearing your socks "jacked up" like that. Jacked-up white socks are especially attractive with a pair of sturdy leather sandals. If I add a sweater, some lederhosen, and braids in my hair, I'm ready to tackle the Alps. My heart sings at the thought:

> *And as I go I love to sing, my knapsack on my back ...*
> *Val da ree! Val da rah! Val da ree!*
> *Val da rah-ha-ha-ha-ha-ha ...*

That last line is a portent of my daughters' reaction if I invited them to jack up their socks and come along: "Ha-ha-ha-ha-ha-ha!"

My sock bin also holds my pantyhose collection. Though I buy my pantyhose twelve matching pairs at a time, online at a deep discount, I seldom have a single intact pair. Every pair is made of two single legs reassembled to make pantyhose.

Here's how it works. When I get a run in one leg of my pantyhose—and the run gets to the point where there's not enough clear nail polish in the world to stop it and it's down to the foot so I can't wear the pantyhose even under pants—I cut off that leg. (The pantyhose leg, just so we are clear.) The next time I get a run in one leg of another pair of pantyhose, I cut off that leg as well. Then I assemble the two tops, slipping one good leg through the hole where the previous bad leg was. How's that for frugality? How's that for confusing?

As a bonus, I get double the control top; it's not quite the industrial strength I need, but close.

Stuffed into the back corner of the closet was my box of "painting clothes." Painting pants, painting shorts, and painting jeans. Painting sweatshirts, painting tees, and painting tank tops. Painting sneakers, painting socks, and painting sandals. How many pieces of clothing could I possibly wear while I was painting? No question I was prepared to paint, in every season, in every climate. (Except the Alps; I was fresh out of painting lederhosen.)

No question that my closet needed a serious overhaul. I'd been neglecting this particular chore for too long. Clearing the closet clutter was long overdue.

(Speaking of overdue, I uncovered a library book that was due so long ago I'd declared it lost and paid for it already. I'd paid for it so long ago that I didn't remember paying for it, until the librarian reminded me the following week when I tried to return it.)

No question about it, my closet needed a serious intervention, and the closet pros all had the same plan:

Step 1: Empty the Closet. (Check!)
Step 2: Sort. One pile for KEEP, a box to DONATE,
         and a big, *big* garbage bag for TRASH. I dug in.

Are you like me? Do you have a pair of way-too-small jeans? These are the jeans that (a) you've saved since high school, or before you had babies, thinking you'll fit into them again someday or (b) you've never actually worn but you bought them as an incentive to stick with that great diet you were absolutely positively going to stick with and lose the weight finally, once and for all time. (That was ten diets ago and you never did fit into the jeans, but you know that someday ... really, you will.)

I took my way-too-small jeans and had a little ceremony as I tossed them into DONATE, singing like the *Sound of Music* von Trapp kids, "So long, farewell, *auf Wiedersehen*, goodbye ..."

So long to "someday I'll ..." Farewell to fantasy. *Auf Wiedersehen* to the awful pressure to be something I'm not. Goodbye and good riddance to unrealistic expectations!

I moved on to my pile of sweatshirts. Three of them were embroidered with the name of a company I used to work for. Every time I think about that job I get the shakes. High pressure. Constant stress. I almost went nuts working there.

I thought those six days would never end.

Why was I hanging on to shirts that brought me back to those stressful times? I decided I needed to dump the shirts and the stressful memories along with them. Into TRASH they went. (I didn't want to donate my stress to anyone else.)

If I need another sweatshirt, I'll get one from someplace calming and serene. The local library, maybe, if they ever declare another amnesty.

The sweatshirts dealt with, I moved on to the lingerie. I found the black "sucker-inner" I bought for a wedding so I could suck enough of me in to fit the had-to-have-it, even-though-it-would-look-better-if-I-lost-ten-pounds, dress I bought. (What's that, you say? You have that same dress?) Sucker-inners are always keepers.

Remember your mother saying, "Be sure to wear decent underwear in case you're ever in an accident"? Looking at my unmentionables, I realized how fortunate the medical community is that I've been accident free. I can imagine the paramedics snickering over my knickers. I imagine the ER staff holding up my baggy raggedy bloomers and hearing them say, as I pass out from embarrassment, "Didn't her mother ever *tell* her?" (Wait till they see my appendix on the X-rays!)

Into TRASH went all the ragged, sagging, worn out drawers, bras, and nightwear. Anything with holes, stretched-out elastic, or frayed edges. Anything gray that used to be white. Anything pink that used to be white. Anything from pregnancy. (How old is the baby? Ten? Twenty?)

I tossed with a vengeance, and in the end I had a couple of bras and four halfway decent pairs of undies left, including the breathing pair. And one gorgeous nightgown my husband gave me several years before as a gift. I'd worn it just once. What was I saving it for? I decided to wear it that night. (The next morning I decided to buy more just like it.)

I tackled my shoe pile next. Same rules: If you love it, wear it, and it's in good shape, KEEP. If you don't love it, or don't wear it but someone else might, DONATE. If it's ragged, TRASH. In the end, I had a pair of flats, a pair of heels, a pair of sandals, and a pair of sneakers left. I'm not a centipede; how many shoes do I really need, anyway?

That was the burning question as I sorted and tossed. How many did I really need? How much of what I thought I needed was really excess? Purchased on impulse or one of those clearance-clearance rack "bargains" that turn out to be huge mistakes? Did I really need eight white T-shirts? Oh sure, each one had a little different style, but in the final analysis, they were eight white T-shirts.

How much time, energy, and money had I wasted over the years, for lack of planning, organizing, and foresight? Ouch!

Sorting and tossing done, I hung up the remains of my wardrobe and, per the expert's advice, arranged the items by color. What a shock! So much black, white, beige, and gray. So little color in my wardrobe, in my life.

The grays, beiges, and blahs reflected my general mood over the past several years. Hormone challenges and life changes had me in and out of the fog of depression; dark days hung with clouds of gloom. But things had changed. It was time for a new life and a more creative way of living. And I wanted my wardrobe to reflect that.

I wanted less beige, more brilliant. Less tan, more terrific. Less dull, more dazzle. I wanted to change my wardrobe ways, to have the outside of me reflect the inside—the fun, vibrant, exciting woman I really am. The fun vibrant woman God created.

Consider the Lilies

"Consider the lilies," Jesus says. God dresses them in splendor. They don't shop till they drop or worry about what they will wear. They don't obsess about their looks. They stand tall and confident, beautiful and God-honoring by being lilies, just as he created them to be.

Looking at my closet, I saw no splendor. I saw dull practicality. Why? Because I was depressed? Because I was frugal? Because focusing too much on our outward appearance is "sinful pride"?

The truth is my closet reflected the dull gray mood and dark gloom of self-doubt that hung over me. The state of my closet was the state of my mind: afraid to let go of the familiar and the predictable, afraid to believe God, and afraid to trust him.

The truth is I harbored a fear, deep down, in the darkest corner of my "closet": the fear that I wasn't lovable, that I wasn't worth anything, that God would never dress me— others, yes, but not me—in splendor. The fear that, to God, I wasn't a lily at all, but a weed.

"Consider how the lilies grow," Jesus says. "Yet I tell you, not even Solomon in all his splendor was dressed like one of these. If that is how God clothes the grass of the field, which is here today, and tomorrow is thrown into the fire,

how much more will he clothe you, O you of little faith!"
(Luke 12:27 – 28).

Clothed in splendor and stunning to behold, lilies are provided for so beautifully, though they are just flowers. The
illustration is not about dressing in finery and spending a fortune on a wardrobe makeover. It's about God's love for his
creation, for his children.

Could God love me that much? If God does that for lilies,
what would he do for me? Could my heavenly Father clothe
me in like fashion, bringing that kind of simple confident
beauty into my life? Could my outer being reflect the beauty
of God within?

O me of little faith! Clearing the clutter from the closet felt
like a first step. I began to see things in a new light.

"Lord," I prayed, "today the sweatshirts. Tomorrow the
soul."

"Do not worry about your life, what you will eat;
or about your body, what you will wear.
Life is more than food, and the body more than clothes."
—Luke 12:22–23

✳✳✳

Points to Ponder

1. Go to your clothes closet. Choose one thing that doesn't fit, doesn't look good, or that you've never liked. Throw it away (or give it away, if you must inflict it on someone else). Get it out of your life today.

2. Continue to toss or recycle one thing in your home every day for the next month. How does it feel to make room in your life?

3. What is cluttering up your spiritual life? What old raggedy thoughts crowd out the fabulous new life God has ready for you? What needs purging? Purge your soul in prayer. What do you sense God saying to you?

✳✳✳

10

Kaflooey

The washer and dryer are in the kitchen. Some people do that on purpose. Not me. My washer and dryer are in the kitchen because we demolished the main-floor laundry room to make space to add a shower to the bathroom next to the laundry. We added the shower because my mother moved from the second floor bedroom to a bedroom on the main floor of our house. (Are you still with me?)

Mother moved to the main floor because she developed occasional vertigo. Vertigo is worrisome when you're going up and down stairs. Especially if you're over ninety.

So the washer and dryer are in the kitchen waiting for the new laundry we're building in part of the garage — all because my mother got dizzy.

My office used to be in that main floor bedroom now occupied by my dizzy mother. I'm temporarily working in the dining room where a canyon of boxes surrounds the table. The box canyon holds fifteen years' worth of writing files, books, reference materials, and assorted memorabilia. I'll work in the dining room until my new office in the basement is completed. Just to be sure you're still with me, let me summarize the chaos:

1. Main floor laundry room demolished; washer and dryer temporarily in kitchen, awaiting new laundry room.
2. Dizzy mother now living in main-floor bedroom, across hall from bathroom-laundry reconstruction project, awaiting new shower.
3. My office temporarily in dining room, awaiting new office in basement.
4. My mind missing in growing pile of debris; sanity in question. Awaiting Jesus' return. Hoping it is soon.

Trying to visualize my mess has probably given *you* vertigo. This would be so much clearer if I could draw you a diagram, like on Monday Night Football. (I'd be the one throwing the Hail Mary pass.)

Meanwhile, in the underworld, creating a new basement work space for me required that we haul fifteen years' worth of stuff (and you know the kind of stuff I mean — nasty mysterious stuff) from the dark recesses of basement storage areas out into the basement family room. It's good my mother wasn't there to see it; we got a little dizzy ourselves, looking at our nasty mysterious stuff all at once.

With all that stuff out of the dark recesses, we got the first good look in fifteen years at the back wall of our basement. The contractor looked too. "Uh-oh ..." he said, looking at the beam where the basement ceiling met the kitchen floor above. If you've ever been involved in a construction or remodeling project, you know that when a contractor says, "Uh-oh," the next sound you'll hear is the *ka-ching!* of the cost going up.

"Your house is sagging," he said, calmly, as if he were saying, "The sky is blue."

"What do you mean?" I said, not so calmly, as if I were saying, "What you mean is the house is sagging and it's going to cost so much to fix it that we'll be bankrupt before you can say 'third mortgage' and I'll have to work until I'm ninety just to be able to eat and my grandchildren can just forget about any inheritance, or even their next birthday presents!"

We really had no choice; a sagging house is never a good thing. The contractor jacked the house up, along with his estimate, and shored up our sagging beam. The beam was sagging less than an inch. We soon discovered the impact that moving one measly beam one measly little inch has on the parts of the house above the beam; in our case, the kitchen.

Cracks in the kitchen drywall. Kitchen cabinets no longer flush against the wall. And twisting in the kitchen window frames; now they can't be removed for easy cleaning. Bummer. And one of those windows no longer locks. (I tell you this without fear; you wouldn't want to come and steal our nasty mysterious stuff. You have enough of your own, don't you?)

The sag was fixed but the mess remained. With the washer and dryer crowding the kitchen, canyons growing in the dining room, stuff stuffing the family room, construction debris flying everywhere, and a layer of dust deepening daily on every horizontal surface (Why clean in the middle of the mess?), all semblance of order in our lives was gone. Chaos reigned.

A friend—a neat orderly friend—came over in the middle of it all. She looked around and said, with a shudder, "I want to run back outside. How can you stand it? It's as if your whole house has gone kaflooey!"

Kaflooey. What a great word. What a perfect description of our home, our routine, and our lives at the moment.

I said it all started because my mother got dizzy, but kaflooey really started before that. She moved in a year before, when living on her own in her apartment became difficult.

She wasn't remembering things like she used to; we became her "assisted living." Mother moved into the guest room upstairs, next to our daughter's room. That's when the kaflooey really started.

Well, actually, it started before that, before my mother needed help, back when our children were moving in and out and in and out after high school—that revolving door period of life with boomerang children. But now that I think about it, kaflooey was happening even before that, when the children were younger and in sports and in school and in Scouts and we were changing careers and getting our finances back under control.

But really, kaflooey was going on earlier than that, when we were first blending our family, moving across the country, and building a new life together. And getting divorced before all that was rather kaflooey-ish as well. And my childhood wasn't exactly kaflooey-free, either, truth be told.

So it's a fact of life: kaflooey occurs. Houses sag. Messes build. Windows stick. Roles shift. Jobs end. Illness strikes. People come. People go. Washers and dryers end up in the kitchen. Kaflooey!

He's Got the Whole World

One morning, in the middle of the kaflooey, I started singing that old song, "He's Got the Whole World in His Hands." I was singing it to God; at least I thought I was. I sang, "You've got the whole world," but when I got to the end of the line I sang, "... in *my* hands." A slip of the tongue, I thought. But as I continued to sing, "You've got my sweet husband ... my dear, dear children ... my itty bitty grandbabies ... my dear old mother," my tongue kept slipping. Each time, I stumbled over "in *my* hands." Each time I prayed the correction, *In* your *hands, Lord ... I meant in* your *hands ... really, I did.*

Didn't I? Not every slip of the tongue is a Freudian slip of deep-seated significance. (Excuse me, Dr. Freud, but my calling my mother-in-law by the dog's name is not a sign of latent hostility. I do the same thing to my children. What's that, you say? Well, maybe I *do* need to lie down for a moment, and your couch does look comfortable. Now about my childhood kaflooey ...)

Maybe most slips of the tongue aren't significant, but this one was. Singing "in *my* hands" wasn't just a slip of the tongue; it was a confession, a statement of my true nature. It was an admission of my desire to have control in life, to have everything in my hands.

In the middle of the kaflooey—present and past—my feelings of frustration and panic come from the realization that things are out of my hands. The realization that I have no control.

The sweet husband has heart trouble; I can't control that. I've prayed and pleaded, begged and bargained to no avail. I have no control over heart disease.

I have no control over my dear, dear grown-up children. I've prayed and pleaded, wheedled and cajoled there too. Again, to no avail. Would I want to control their lives? Don't I have enough trouble controlling my own?

Those itty bitty grandbabies? Well, they have their own lives with their own parents who have their own lives. Let their parents do the wheedling and cajoling for them and with them. Let their parents find out for themselves that they don't have any control. That torch has passed.

My dear old mother? I can't control her present or her future. I've prayed and pleaded about her too, but I can't change the fact that she's got dementia. I can't control the need she has for care, or the losses the disease brings. Or the grief I'm feeling.

I can't control any of this, so I trust God. I trust God because I have no other choice.

But what about myself? I sing about myself this way (and do more often than I like to admit): "I've got *my* plans for *my* future in *my* hands." I want to control my future. Of course, I want God to be in charge of limiting the amount of future kaflooey that comes my way, but I want to be able to make my plans and have my plans succeed. I'll "give" God the big stuff, the stuff involving other people, the stuff I know I can't control, but when it comes to "my" stuff, I want to be in charge. I'll leave others and eternity up to God, but I want things in my temporal earthly life to be the way I want them to be. I want them to be in *my* hands, under *my* control.

But control is just an illusion, isn't it? God's in charge. He decides. I can make all the plans I want, but he is the one who decides what's going to happen. I am not in control. Not really. Not ever.

How exhausting it is to try to hold it all in my hands. How exhausting to try to control everything, to worry, to fret, to fuss. "Let go," God says. "Let go."

In His Hands

Escaping from the kaflooey for a moment, I step out onto the porch, plop down in a wicker chair, and look out into the woods. The late-afternoon sun lights the pines. A cool breeze stirs the poplars. A chipmunk, cheeks bulging with black oil seed from our bird feeder, disappears into a hole in a red oak.

Looking at creation, I sense the bigness of God, the immensity of his power keeping the universe in motion. He does have the whole of creation in his hands.

But the forest, like life, is not tidy. Untamed brambles and thick brush grow from a mat of decomposing leaves and fallen limbs. It's a mess, assaulted by wind, burned by sun, drenched by rain.

The forest is a mess — quite kaflooey-ish actually — but underneath the mess there is a plan. Divine order assigns a purpose and a time for everything.

God is the constant in the chaos. His ever-watching eye sees all — the minor frustrations and the major pains in life. He sees the canyons and the chaos, the dark mysterious stuff of suffering. He sees us there, lost, confused, alone, and afraid. In the middle of kaflooey, whatever ours might be, he whispers, "Breathe. Watch. Wait. Remember."

Our kaflooey, whatever it might be, is temporary. This current mess won't last forever. Eventually — the contractor promised! — things will be settled. The canyons will disappear. The chaos will be calmed. The dark stuff will be brought into the light.

Eventually, Mother will be in her new room. The washer and dryer will be in the new laundry room in the garage. I'll be able to get to the stove again. (Oh goody.)

But for this moment on the porch, I breathe in the warm afternoon and remember that God ordains the sunset and the moonrise. He keeps the planets spinning. He directs the chipmunks. As I wait for order to return to my home, he offers calm for my soul. I remember that he is the unchanging everlasting God. I remember what he has given me — love and life eternal. Nothing else seems as important in this moment as I dare to trust.

He has everything under control. He's got the whole world ... the sweet, sweet family ... the itty bitty babies ... the dear old folks ... and yes, you and me, sister ... in his hands. He's got the whole world in his hands.

In the middle of kaflooey, he offers us respite from the mess. He offers us moments of peace.

> But as for me, it is good to be near God.
> I have made the Sovereign LORD my refuge;
> I will tell of all your deeds.
> —Psalm 73:28

Points to Ponder

1. Describe a construction or remodeling project you've been involved in. Did everything go according to plan? What was the biggest challenge for you? What do you wish you'd known then that you know now?

2. What kind of kaflooey are you dealing with right now? What helps you cope? What doesn't?

3. Where do you find respite from the mess of life? Describe that special place.

11

A New Atti-toot

You know you've given birth to a Strong Willed Child (or SWC) when, in the delivery room, your newborn looks up at you as if to say, "Thanks for the ride, Mom. I'll take it from here!" And she does.

Katy, my second-born, was my SWC; she followed three years after her cooperative and compliant older brother. I've heard other parents say, "If the SWC had been my *first* child, that would have been my *only* child!" Amen! Child-free friends tell me that babysitting for the SWC is a very effective means of birth control.

Katy, eager to expand her havoc-raising horizons, learned to crawl early; it was her first sport. When her dad's employer offered a crawling contest at a company picnic, Katy won first place, beating several other infants in her class as she crawled for all she was worth to score the plastic Donald Duck bank at the end of the track. Hugging the bank, she turned and smiled—gloated, I swear—at the other babies.

At home, she zoomed up the stairs before I could close the baby gate. She was a flash, emptying cupboards and drawers as fast as I could fill them back up. She was still tiny when she figured out how to climb out of her crib, which she did dozens of times each evening, refusing to go to sleep until the last of the grown-ups was out for the night. The SWC is truly a party animal.

"Pick your battles" became my motto; with the SWC, *everything* is a battle. While Katy's peers delighted their parents with "da-da" and "ma-ma," her first word was "No!"(I've heard that SWCs assume their name must be "No!" since they hear it so early and so often.) We said, "No!" and quickly realized that the SWC dictionary defines *No!* as "Go ahead and try it again to see if they really meant it!"

For instance, she loved messing with the adjustments on the television. I'd calmly remove her from the temptation, distracting her with her toys. Back she'd go. "No!" I'd say, removing and distracting again. "No!" she'd say right back to me and return to fiddling with the TV. Around and around we'd go, with me distracting and her fiddling. Three times. Four times. Ten. Twenty. It was a test of wills, and the SWC would *not* back down. Neither could I.

The first full sentence Katy put together was, "I can't like it!"

"Here's some macaroni and cheese," I'd say.

"I can't like it!" she'd say.

"How about some chicken?" I'd say.

"I can't like it!" she'd say.

"How about some ice cream?" I'd say. Ha! Two could play her little game.

She'd fix me with a steely eye and say, with an eerie calm and a cunning little smile, slowly, as if *she* were the one explaining things to a two year old, "I ... can't ... like ... it."

One day my mother was visiting our house, and Katy, still a toddler, was "helping" unpack a bag of canned goods I'd picked up at the store. She held a soup can in her little hand and eyed the dog; she looked ready to heave the soup in the pup's direction. "Put the can down, Katy," I said. (I shuddered with a sudden fast-forward, imagining her in the future with the police saying, "Just put the weapon down, lady, and nobody gets hurt.")

Katy looked at me and said, "Shut up, dummy!" And then she spat—*ptooey!*—in my direction. My mother, witnessing the exchange, stifled a laugh.

"You think that's funny?" I demanded.

"No, but I was thinking that she's just like you were!" My mother had that look of satisfaction that comes only with long-awaited payback. Revenge was sweet, it seemed.

Just like me? I was shocked. *Moi? A Strong Willed Child?* How could my mother say that? I'd always been so well-behaved and so cooperative. I'd always been such a good girl! Except for those times when I wanted my own way, which was most of the time. Except for those times when someone wanted me to do what I didn't want to do, which was the rest of the time. *Hmm.*

What goes around, comes around, they say. God says we reap what we sow. I had to admit it; Katy and I were two peas in a pod, the nut hadn't fallen far from the tree, and every other cliche. She inherited my strong-willed nature and ramped it up tenfold. I prayed we'd both survive her childhood.

As Katy got older and more "reasonable," we'd discuss her behavior. At length. *Ad nauseum.* One day, when she was about six, she and I discussed her recent antics. After pretending to listen to what I had to say, she put one hand up, palm toward me in a dismissive gesture, as in "Yada, yada, yada, blah, blah, blah ... I've heard it all before," and then looked me in the eye—again with that wily look of cold steel—and said, "I know, I *know*! I need a new *atti-toot*!"

At least she didn't spit this time.

Atti-toot! Oh yes, she had one and she needed a new one! And she knew it, even at the tender age of six. I suspect she'd known it from birth. It was nice to hear her admit it.

It's All about Atti-toot!

Ninety percent of life is atti-toot, isn't it? Chuck Swindoll says, "I am convinced that life is ten percent what happens to me and ninety percent how I react to it. And so it is with you. We are in charge of our attitude."

It's our choice. We can gripe, or we can grow. We can bemoan, or we can believe. We can complain, or we can conquer. It's our choice.

We can moan about the manure, or we can start looking for the pony. It's all about attitude.

Writers I've known have taught me a useful attitude: "Bad things don't happen to writers. It's all just material." When we find ourselves in that twister game of life, we tell ourselves, *This is all just material . . . I'll write about this someday.* That attitude gives us the emotional distance we need to be able to do the reporting.

"It's all just material" lets us make our mental notes at the accident scene; we're there, but we're elsewhere at the same time. "It's all just material" means we are in the back row at the funeral mourning and, at the same time, making notes about the setting, the flowers, and the sounds. We record our impressions, filing them away for later processing. The mourners might become the basis for the characters in our future novel. The experience might be the foundation of a future article on grief. (Or an article on good manners, in which case we are the example of what *not* to do at a funeral.)

"It's all just material," we tell ourselves, after rescuing our three-year-old SWC who has scaled the inner ladderlike branches of a thirty foot pine just for the joy of proudly bellowing, "Look, Mommy! I'm high!" (We shudder again, imagining the daredevil's future. And the police involvement.)

With her safe return to earth, we catch our breath, and when our hearts stop thumping, we capture the experience in our ever-present notebook. "It's all just material," we tell ourselves again, because it cushions us from the feelings we don't want to feel yet. The terror of seeing. The heartache of hearing. The worry of the what-ifs. Writing gives us a place to process those feelings later, after the terror has passed and we've gained some perspective. (Twenty-plus years later, in the SWC's case.)

I've reassured my fainting heart that it's all just material a thousand times. It's been my attitude of choice. You're holding the by-product of that attitude in your hands, the stories of life and love and loss, of change and challenge, all of it "material" delivered to this writer from the hand of her loving Father in heaven. The pain, the sorrow, the joy, the triumph—it's all been allowed by him for purposes beyond my understanding.

Bad things do happen to writers, of course. But I choose to look at it as material—the material of life, allowed by God and passing through me to you.

Attitude is the only thing we can control in this life, isn't it? We can't control the things that happen to us; we can control only our reaction to them. Swindoll puts it this way: "The remarkable thing is we have a choice every day regarding the attitude we will embrace for that day. We cannot change our past. We cannot change the fact that people will act in a certain way. We cannot change the inevitable. The only thing we can do is play on the one string we have, and that is our attitude."

Attitude is our choice; often it is the only choice we have. The attitude we choose will affect how well we adjust to change and challenge. The attitude we choose will impact how we cope with grief and despair. The attitude we choose will determine how we handle the things that come our way—whether they will overwhelm us, or we will triumph over them.

Eating the Bread

There is a story of the triumph of attitude in the Old Testament, where we find Caleb at the age of eighty-five asking to be awarded the land of the Anakites as his own. The Anakites were people "of great stature," of fierce reputation and feared by many. But Caleb had no fear, for he had chosen his attitude *forty years earlier.* Forty years earlier, when everyone else feared confronting these giants, Caleb suggested courage: "Neither fear ye the people of the land; for they are bread for us" (Numbers 14:9 KJV).

Author Watchman Nee offers this take on Caleb's attitude. "He sought to show the children of Israel that in the land itself there were resources upon which they could draw in order to possess it. 'The people of the land ... are bread for us,' he declared. What is bread? Bread is something you eat. Bread is something that brings increased strength. Every time you meet a difficulty, every time you find yourself in an impossible situation, ask yourself this question: Am I going to starve here, or am I going to eat the food that is set before me? If you are relying on the Lord for victory and let his overcoming life be manifested in you, you will find nourishment and increased vitality in accepting as 'bread' those obstacles that are contesting your progress."

Challenge is bread. Trouble is bread. Adversity is bread. Illness is bread. Grief is bread. Resistance and fear and misery are choices we make. Acceptance and courage and peace are choices too.

"The Lord is with us; fear them not," Caleb said. Caleb, choosing an attitude of focusing on God's presence and power, saw things differently. Do you see that, because the Lord is with us, we can see trouble, in whatever form it comes, differently?

Because the Lord is with us, trouble becomes a teacher, offering lessons in gratitude. We stop taking our blessings for granted. *(Our home was spared from the tornado. No more complaints about leaking faucets!)*

Trouble brings perspective. When illness threatens life, our spouse's irritating little habits don't bug us as much. *(I'll be glad to pick up his dirty socks from now to eternity because he's still here to wear them!)*

Trouble builds character. It is true in life that "what doesn't kill you makes you stronger." Because the Lord is with us, we can confront the enemy—the enemy without or the enemy within—and that process builds spiritual character. In the process, regardless of the outcome, our faith grows stronger. In the process, regardless of the result, our trust increases. In the process, our appreciation for God's love, faithfulness, and mercy grows.

As a result of this character-building process, we become less self-reliant and more God-reliant. Depending less on self and more on God, we are stronger, more merciful, more gracious, and more compassionate. Having been loved through trouble, we love more readily. Have received so much, we are open to giving more.

Because the Lord is with us, trouble is "bread" for sustenance and growth. Because the Lord is with us, trouble becomes the fuel to power needed change in our lives and in our hearts.

One thing is certain in life: trouble will come. Our only choice will be our reaction to it—our attitude. We can choose to cower in fear, defeated before we even engage in battle, or we can choose to go boldly forward, trusting that, because the Lord is with us, we will be stronger in the end.

Trouble takes many forms in this life. Sometimes it comes as a cherub with blue eyes, blond curls, a mischievous smile, and a whole lot of attitude. I see now that having such "trouble with an atti-toot" forced me to adjust my own attitudes.

Through trouble, God humbled this mother, who thought she had all the answers, and taught her to pray. Through trouble, God taught this mother to trust him for the future of her children. Through trouble, God taught this mother—who needed so badly to know it—what unconditional love is all about.

God sent trouble to me, and I wouldn't have it any other way. Through trouble, God enriched my life and nourished my heart in ways beyond imagining. And trouble continues to bless me, to this very day.

> The Lord says, "I will rescue those who love me.
> I will protect those who trust in my name.
> When they call on me, I will answer;
> I will be with them in trouble.
> I will rescue them and honor them."
> —Psalm 91:14–15 (NLT)

＊＊＊＊＊＊＊＊＊＊＊＊＊＊＊＊＊＊＊＊＊＊＊＊＊＊＊＊＊＊＊＊＊＊

Points to Ponder

1. Do you know a Strong Willed Child? What is the biggest challenge with this SWC? What is the greatest blessing? What has God taught you through your experience?

2. Describe a time when you were afraid of a challenge or lived in fear of what the future might bring. How did you handle it? What did you learn?

3. What "atti-toot" of yours gets in the way of contentment and peace? Are you stubborn or rebellious? Are you fearful or shy? How would a change of attitude benefit you? What action can you take to change?

＊＊＊＊＊＊＊＊＊＊＊＊＊＊＊＊＊＊＊＊＊＊＊＊＊＊＊＊＊＊＊＊＊＊

12

Of Mice and Women

A delightful children's book begins, "If you give a mouse a cookie, he'll want a glass of milk ..." The mouse requires more and more attention, in a circle of frustration and demand that ends where it began, "He's going to want a glass of milk." Cute mouse, charming story.

Not my mouse. Not my story.

We saw the first mouse two weeks after we moved into our house in the woods. The house had been vacant for two years because, according to the realtor, "This is too far out in the country for most local people." We laughed. The house was a fifteen-minute drive from town. We'd just moved to Wisconsin from southern California, where fifteen minutes gets you nowhere.

But this vacant country house was not vacant. A mouse had taken up residence. Terry spotted it on a Sunday morning in the basement family room just before we left for church. I was upstairs in the kitchen when I heard him holler.

"Mouse!" Yelling "Mouse!" is like screaming "Fire!" It gets everyone's attention.

"Mouse? Where? Where's a mouse?" The kids came thundering from all corners of the house.

"Get the broom!" Terry yelled to me.

"Get the *cats*!" my son yelled to his sisters.

Our two cats, Domino and Tigger, were southern California cats and accustomed to climate-controlled, indoor living. They were unaccustomed to being around wild creatures, other than the children.

Our cats had never even been outdoors except for the time that Tigger wandered outside accidentally. She spent an hour hiding under the rhododendrons next to the foundation, meowing loudly for rescue. Her tiny paws had evidently never felt dirt or wood chips. The poor dear couldn't cope.

Back in the family room, Terry grabbed the broom and used it to coax the mouse toward the now-open sliding glass door. I offered encouragement.

"Shoo, shoo, little mouse," I said. Terry offered words of advice as well—not nearly as gentle as mine. The mouse, preferring his cozy basement abode to the chilly outdoors, ran toward the couch. The cats, curiosity aroused, loped toward him. The mouse froze in place, six inches from safety, as the cats stared at him.

Moments passed as I wondered if these domesticated felines might still possess some primeval urge to hunt. Apparently not. They stared at the possum-playing mouse, and then turned their noses up and sauntered away in true cat fashion, with tails high as if to say, "*Bo*-ring! This can't be something to eat. Food comes in a bag."

Mousey skedaddled under the couch. We left for church, shutting the door to the family room with the mouse and the two cats trapped inside. We hoped that the cats would eventually get the idea. A few hours later, we returned to find a dead mouse and Domino and Tigger sitting guard over it, daring it to move again.

"Eww!" said the daughters.

"Cool!" said the son.

"Good kitties!" said Terry.

"Poor little mouse," said I.

That particular mouse battle was over, but the war had just begun, for our house, we soon realized, had become a mouse mecca in its two vacant years.

The invasion called for desperate measures. I learned how to set traps. I had never laid a trap for any living creature in my life. (As a child, while my brothers delighted in frying ants under the magnifying glass, I caught ants, put them in empty glass jars, named them, and tried to train them. I was so proud of my ants "learning" to climb sticks.)

So against my better nature, I set traps, using peanut butter for bait. Mice love peanut butter, I'd heard. At first I cringed at the thought of killing, but it turns out that I, far more than the cats, possessed a primeval urge to hunt. Soon I was laying trap lines and checking them every morning like a voyageur after pelts.

The war escalated. Oh, how those little critters breed! I became a spy, listening at the walls for noises in the night, lying still in bed to identify the precise pattern of the scurrying in the attic above the bedroom. Were they traveling along ceiling joists, or was it the furnace ductwork they followed?

Briefings over breakfast became routine as Terry and the children joined the battle. "I heard scratching above the bathroom sink last night," the son reported one morning.

"I heard it in my bedroom ceiling," a daughter said.

"Me too," said the other.

"Put some poison in the attic today," Colonel Terry ordered.

"Roger that," said Major Mom. We fought long and hard. Sometimes we felt that victory was in our grasp. And then we'd find a slew of traps, unsprung but licked clean of peanut butter. Not only were our mice living, but they were living well.

I started mixing the peanut butter with poison pellets for the traps. (I'm ashamed to confess the maniacal glee that gave me. If you give a mouse a cookie, he'll want a glass of milk; if you give a mouse poisoned peanut butter, he'll die. *Ha! Take that, filthy vermin!*)

The battle raged inside and out. We searched out and filled every hole we could find outside in our old cedar siding. Frustrated that mice were still getting in, we tore off some old siding and there we found Mouse Central Station—huge holes where water damage had rotted away the interior of the wall. To compound the problem, carpenter ants had gotten under the siding in this old house, eating away wider and wider access for the marauding mice.

The mice and ants had combined forces to defeat us. It was time to call in the heavy artillery. Pete the Pest Terminator arrived—a grizzled man with blood in his eye and a tank the size of Cleveland slung over his back. As I opened the door, he leaned down to snuff out his cigar on my front steps, then tucked the stub into his shirt pocket, behind the embroidered *Terminator.*

"You called about bugs?"

"Yes, and mice too."

"I'll start outside and spray the perimeter," Pete said, swinging the toxic tank up so I could see what he'd be using. I didn't want to know. I suddenly pitied the carpenter ants. Perhaps I could catch them in a jar and train them to go to someone else's house.

Fifteen minutes later, Pete came back to report that our perimeter was secured. He showed me a stack of black triangular boxes. For the mice, he explained. "They're attracted to what's inside. They eat it and . . ." He must have seen me close my eyes and grimace. I, who had been trapping and killing for months, suddenly felt queasy.

"Let's just say," he gave a wicked little laugh, exposing his few remaining nicotine-stained teeth, "it's hazardous to their health. Which way to the basement?" I pointed. He headed down the stairs to distribute the black boxes of death.

Week after week, Pete brought in the heavy artillery. I continued to set my traps, and the numbers of enemy casualties climbed significantly. The ants—and every other kind of bug—disappeared from a four-foot perimeter outside our foundation wall. The walls grew quiet. The ceiling scurries ceased. An occasional whiff of decaying mouse hit us from within the recesses of our walls, but the temporary nastiness was worth it.

After months of enemy occupation, Pete certified us to be pest free. We were at peace.

Peace lasted a year. Then one morning while cleaning my office I discovered, in a hidden corner behind my desk, a pile of dry cat food. Marauding midnight mice had stashed it in there, no question. I called the Colonel's office immediately.

"Mickey's back," I said. He knew the code.

"I'll bring home traps and poison," he said. "And you'd better call Pete."

"Roger that."

Like a World War II air-raid warden, I'm ever vigilant, scanning the floors for the first sign of scat, listening in the walls for initial stirrings, alert to skittering across the attic joists. Ever vigilant for signs that the enemy has returned.

And I need to be vigilant because the first mouse is never the last mouse.

I'm here to tell you: If you give a mouse a cookie, he won't just want a glass of milk. He'll invite all his friends and his vast extended family to join him. They'll invade your basement, your attic, your walls and your closets. They'll eat your wiring, chew your insulation, and eventually make you sick.

Pete said it best. "Don't let the first mouse in." Great advice. And it applies to more than furry rodents. It applies to life. I dare not say, "Oh well, it's just one little mouse. It's not hurting anything." I know what happens next. I know the destruction that follows.

First Mice

I can't say, "Oh it's just one little brownie," because I know me. One little brownie leads me to another slightly less-little brownie. And another. Before I know it, I've got my face in a whole pan of brownies, and cake, and ice cream, and cookies, and all the other wonderful, fabulous sweet treats I crave, and then ... *Where was I? Oh yeah* ... Before I know it, I've lost my way instead of the weight. (Perhaps you can have the one little brownie and be satisfied. I can't.)

I can't say, "Oh it's just one little cigarette," if I really want to be a nonsmoker. I can't say, "Oh it's just one little drink," if sobriety is my goal.

I know the destruction that follows, how one little thing can become one huge problem.

One little lie, one little compromise, one little lapse of judgment has the potential to destroy my integrity and my reputation.

One little foray to the casino, to the porn site, to the dark side can destroy my relationships, my future, and eventually my faith.

But, oh! The temptation to indulge, to allow, or to rationalize just that one little thing. Just this once. The temptation to ignore that little voice—Is it conscience? Is it Pete?—that says, "Don't do it. Don't let the first mouse in."

The problem is that "once" too easily becomes "twice." Allowing one slip makes it easier to allow another and then another.

We must be ever vigilant. Vigilant in deciding what we will allow in—into our homes, into our heads, or into our hearts. The Bible warns, "Be self-controlled and alert. Your enemy the devil prowls around like a roaring lion looking for someone to devour" (1 Peter 5:8). Temptation—just that one little thing—is all around. But there is good news:

"The temptations in your life are no different from what others experience. And God is faithful. He will not allow the temptation to be more than you can stand. When you are tempted, he will show you a way out so that you can endure" (1 Corinthians 10:13 NLT).

How often we allow the mice to overrun our lives, and then blame God for not helping us resist the temptation! At least I've done that. How about you?

The time for me to resist the brownies is not when I'm looking at the pan, still warm from the oven, holding the knife in my hand, ready to slice into that heavenly delight. The time to resist is not when I'm combining the ingredients in the bowl. The time to resist is before that. I can't let the first mouse—or in this case, brownie mix—into my shopping cart. God will show me (if I let him) the way out; it's usually through the produce department!

The time to resist the drink is not when you have the booze or the wine in the glass. The time to resist is not when you are reaching for the bottle in the cupboard. The time to resist is not when you are standing in the store in front of the shelves of liquor. The time to resist the temptation to drink is long before that. Ask God to show you the way out of addiction.

The time to think about maintaining your sexual purity is not when you are alone in the moonlight in the car, parked with that dreamy someone. The time to resist the temptation to start smoking again is not when you've got the cigarette in your mouth and the matches in your hand. The time to resist the urge to gamble is not when you're sitting at the slot machine.

You get the idea. Don't let the first mouse in. Ask God to show you the way out, the way to resist, the way of escape.

What are the mice in your life? What mouse is tempting you and threatening your peace of heart right now? Action, attitude, or addiction—ask God to show you healthier, safer, saner alternatives. Ask God to show you how to plug the holes where the mice are getting in.

Ask God to "mouse-proof" your life today. He can give you peace—if you will let him.

Submit yourselves, then, to God.
Resist the devil, and he will flee from you.
Come near to God and he will come near to you.
—James 4:7–8

* *

Points to Ponder

1. Describe a time of "war" in your past. What were you battling? What was the outcome? What did you learn?

2. What temptation is hardest for you to resist today? Overeating? Procrastination? Addiction? What does *vigilance* mean to you? Ask God to help you devise a strategy to resist. Take a positive first step today.

3. With whom, or with what, do you need to make peace today? Take some time in prayer or journaling, expressing your feelings and asking God for release and healing.

* *

13

I've Got It Coming

Picture this scene from Disney's 1930s cartoon "Moving Day." (No, dear children, I was not there for its theatrical premiere; I saw it on television, much, much later!) Mickey and Donald haven't paid their rent in weeks. The sheriff is coming to evict them. They have to move out of the house — fast! (The 1930s audience could relate. Bankruptcies, home foreclosures, and court-mandated evictions executed by the local sheriff were commonplace during that Depression era.)

Onto the screen comes Goofy, the ice man, flapping down the street, singing, "Oh, the world owes me a livin'."

What kind of attitude was that to have during such hard times? Gainfully employed and taking it for granted, Goofy was blessed and oblivious.

Goofy's song was originally from another Disney short, "The Grasshopper and the Ants." You no doubt remember Aesop's familiar fable of the grasshopper who preferred to play the summer away, while the industrious ants labored hard and long to prepare for the coming winter.

"The world owes me a living." Aesop illustrated the attitude. Disney brought it to the big screen. Goofy gave us its "human" face, as he sang, "Oh, the world owes me a livin'."

Fast-forward a couple of decades in America and picture this scene from my childhood. My father is sick with cancer. He's been self-employed for years, a self-taught electrician, plumber, and carpenter with a gift for building and remodeling. Now he is too sick to work. My mother has taken a job cleaning offices at night in downtown Minneapolis. Ends won't meet. My parents have no choice: they apply for "welfare." Aid to Families with Dependent Children, or AFDC, provides a monthly stipend and food supplements.

And my father hates being "on the dole," as he called it. Like so many of his generation, he is proud and fiercely self-reliant. He takes the "handout" because he must, for our sakes, but he doesn't like it one bit. The world doesn't owe *him* a living. He certainly doesn't feel he "has it coming."

He doesn't feel entitled to it; he feels ashamed.

I've Got It Coming!

Goofy sang, "Oh, the world owes me a livin'," and my dad called it shameful. Today we call it the entitlement mentality. Entitlement is the attitude that someone, or maybe everyone, owes me something. Maybe it's born of prosperity, afflicting those of us who are blessed and oblivious. I hate to admit it, but it creeps into my attitude all too often. See if you recognize the signs.

For instance, I've thought at times on the job that the boss owes me not just a paycheck but privileges, understanding, time off when I want it, and forgiveness—a second, third, tenth chance for messing up. The boss and the company are lucky to have me; they owe *me* for showing up every day to work. (How quickly I forget how grateful I was to be hired in the first place. How quickly I start to feel put upon when asked to do the job I was hired to do!)

The company owes me other perks too. Free internet access and time to do my personal surfing and online shopping (when I'm not playing online solitaire). Free postage for my personal mail, unlimited access for my personal email. Free coffee and maybe donuts too. Free parking and on-site child care.

Why stop there? My coworkers and I are entitled to a workplace gym, with a sauna. An on-site cafeteria, with menu options for vegans, lacto-ovos, and beefaholics, as well as those on Atkins, Mediterranean, Zone, Fat Flush, South Beach, GI, and Weight Watchers. Anyone on an "e-diet" is, of course, entitled to more personal internet time during the work day. And to eat at her work station.

We're entitled to birthday cakes and holiday parties—just to be fair, a party for every holiday celebrated by anyone on the payroll. (Or we could combine everything into one big bash: "Happy Cinco-de-Kwan-Hanu-Mas! And a Merry East-Kippur-Madan to all!")

We're entitled to bonuses, paid vacation time, comp time, overtime, double time, and sick time. We are entitled to time off for personal crises, of course—such as needing to leave early to avoid the traffic on a holiday weekend. Or needing to come in late because our favorite store had early-bird specials that morning.

Speaking of shopping, we are also entitled to take home— the company can afford it and nobody is going to miss it—a few pens and some paperclips. Some staples and sticky notes. Rolls of tape and a tape dispenser. A few file folders. An occasional ream of paper. A couple of toner cartridges. It adds up to grand theft office, but who's counting? Besides, we have it coming!

Yes, I've got it coming, not just on the job but on the home front as well. My children owe me. I gave them food and shelter, after all. I'm therefore entitled to have them at my beck and call, running my errands, doing my home repairs (never mind that they have their own home to tend to now), and fetching my slippers.

I'm entitled to have them listen while I complain about the sorry state of the world; to listen as I regale them with tales of yore that all start with, "When I was your age ..."; and to tolerate my endless recitation of everything that ails me. (And after all those hours I spent in labor just to bring them into this sorry world, the *least* they could do is call me once in a while!)

Yes, I've got all that coming from the job, from the family, and from life. And so much more. Amnesty, not fines, for overdue library books. Warnings instead of speeding tickets. Free lunches. Double coupon days. Unlimited credit. No waiting lines. Immediate service. Immediate answers. Immediate access. Free wi-fi and coffee on every corner. You name it and I've got it coming. Just because.

Good grief! When did I start thinking that the world owes me everything I want, right now, right here? (Certainly not from my parents!) Where did this entitlement mindset come from then?

Perhaps it's because this world is populated by haves and have-nots. It has ever been thus, but today, thanks to the immediacy of the media running 24-7 on a gazillion channels, we are more painfully aware of the gap between us and them. Shouldn't the rich and famous be required to share with the poor and anonymous? If everyone just shared equally, we'd all have enough. Wouldn't we? (It's not fair, after all, that someone else has so much money and I have so little. Where is Robin Hood when I need him?)

Or maybe "I've got it coming!" started before cable television. Maybe it began at the beginning.

The Manna Department

Maybe that "I've got it coming" attitude started in Eden. Eve looked at the forbidden fruit and saw that it was "good for food and pleasing to the eye, and also desirable for gaining wisdom" (Genesis 3:6). How it must have appealed: taste, beauty, and power. All her cravings satisfied with one bite. (Can you imagine?) Eve might have felt she was entitled. Eve believed the lie. The Bible makes it clear: "The lust of the flesh, and the lust of the eyes, and the pride of life" are "not of the Father, but is of the world" (1 John 2:16 KJV).

Eve fell. We fell with her. Did the fall hardwire us with the entitlement mentality? Has the "I've got it coming" attitude been here all along?

Later, during their forty years in the desert, God provided for his wandering children, including all that manna. Did they start to feel entitled after a while? Did they take the blessings for granted? Yes. The message in the manna was this: "Remember how the LORD your God led you through the wilderness for these forty years, humbling you and testing you to prove your character, and to find out whether or not you would obey his commands. Yes, he humbled you by letting you go hungry and then feeding you with manna, a food previously unknown to you and your ancestors. He did it to teach you that people do not live by bread alone; rather, we live by every word that comes from the mouth of the Lord" (Deuteronomy 8:2–3 NLT).

God's point in his provision was to humble his people and to teach them. To let them be hungry and then to feed them, so they'd understand that he was the source of everything they needed. Did they learn? Were they humbled? They certainly grumbled.

God's been running the Manna Department since the beginning. Have we taken him for granted? Do we feel entitled to his blessings? My dad's attitude—not expecting anything unless you work for it—wasn't such a bad attitude. But carried too far, such self-reliance becomes a stubborn refusal, for pride's sake, to admit need. He refused to admit that he—and his children—needed help. Instead of graciously accepting the blessing, he let it destroy his spirit.

That kind of self-reliance isn't admirable; it's foolish. "You may say to yourself, 'My power and the strength of my hands have produced this wealth for me.' But remember the LORD your God, for it is he who gives you the ability to produce wealth" (Deuteronomy 8:17–18).

God's been providing for me from day one. Am I humbled? I certainly grumble. Like Eve, I tend to want what I want, and want it now. Like the Israelites, I start to feel, as God provides, that I am entitled to be provided for. Like the Prodigal Son, I want my inheritance. Now.

Like Goofy, secure and warm and well-fed, I am too often blessed and oblivious, taking my blessings for granted and thinking I'm entitled to more. How about you?

I'm so like the grasshopper. I want to play now. I hope summer will never end. But winter always comes. A day of reckoning is coming when my choices will be weighed. The Bible makes it plain that in that day, God "will give to each person according to what he has done" (Romans 2:6). If I let that attitude of entitlement rule my heart, on that day the scales of my life will weigh heavily on the side of selfishness.

There will be a reckoning, and I'll have it coming.

How much have I taken compared with how much I've given? Jesus said, "Give, and it will be given to you. A good measure, pressed down, shaken together and running over, will be poured into your lap. For with the measure you use, it will be measured to you" (Luke 6:38), and, "Freely you have received, freely give" (Matthew 10:8).

Like Eve, like the desert wanderers, like the prodigal—we have received freely from the hand of a loving Father. We've received grace, provision, talent, and countless other blessings. We are called to give as freely as we have taken.

"But what have I to give?" you might protest. None of us has anything to share except what we've received from God. Most of us have nothing fancy, nothing spectacular. But every one of us has the gift of connection with other human beings. We can't give that gift if we are always and only concerned with what we can get from others, focused on what we think the world owes us.

We are not entitled to anything. "Who has ever given to God, that God should repay him?" (Romans 11:35). God owes us nothing. He gives us today. We are not entitled to tomorrow.

We have only today, only this moment really. And this moment is all that we need. A moment to pray, a moment to smile. A moment to praise, a moment to encourage. A moment to decide that, should we be given more moments, more days, and more years, we will spend them wisely, concerned not with what we can get but how we can give.

Give me neither poverty nor riches,
but give me only my daily bread.
Otherwise, I may have too much and disown you
and say, "Who is the LORD?"
Or I may become poor and steal,
and so dishonor the name of my God.
—Proverbs 30:8–9

❋❋

Points to Ponder

1. The Bible says, "It is more blessed to give than to receive" (Acts 20:35). What kind of giver are you? What kind of a receiver are you?

2. Have you ever received "charity"? What were the circumstances? How did it feel?

3. What can you give today? Can you write or speak a word of encouragement, of thanks, of praise, or of love? Someone out there needs what you have to give today.

❋❋

14

Temper, Temper

What does a nice Christian woman, devoted wife and mother, author, speaker, humorist, and all-around fun person know about anger? Plenty.

I remember one Saturday morning when we lived in California. Those were our Brady Bunch days, when I was trying so hard to be the perfect wife, the perfect mother, and the perfect stepmother. All six of our combined children, who ranged from five to thirteen, were in the house that morning.

I had been working all week at a local investment firm, studying for my business degree at night, and taking care of the family. On Friday night after dinner, I'd enlisted the family in helping me clean the whole house. I went to bed late that night, satisfied that the house was perfect.

I slept in Saturday morning. (I was pooped. Who wouldn't be?) When I finally dragged myself out of bed, I went into the kitchen for my coffee. There on the kitchen counter lay a knife smeared with peanut butter and jelly. A nice mom would take something like that in stride. Something like that, a nice mom would pick up and put in the dishwasher if she were lucky enough to have a dishwasher. A nice mom might later explain patiently to the children the importance of everyone working together to keep the house clean.

But I wasn't a nice mom that morning, as I felt a sudden surge of silent rage. *Who ruined my perfect kitchen? One of those children, no doubt.* I had no thought whatsoever that a nice mom would have been up early, making a batch of homemade buttermilk pancakes rather than leaving her little ones to fend for themselves with PB&J.

I had no thought that, with six kids in the house, it was amazing that this was the only thing out of place. I had no thought that I should be relieved that nothing was on fire and nobody was bleeding while I slept in. No, I felt no regret, no remorse, and no relief. I felt only rage.

I picked up that knife and marched down the hall to the back bedroom where I knew the children were all playing, as I built up a full head of angry steam. *These kids don't have any* respect *for me! They don't* appreciate *all I do around here! They don't* care *that I work* all *week and* every *night and* all *weekend just to keep things going around here* ... blah, blah, blah. If you've ever gotten mad at the family for not appreciating you, you know what I was thinking.

On I stomped, getting angrier and angrier, until halfway down the hall when I caught my reflection in a full-length mirror. I stopped dead and sucked in my breath in shock. *Who* is *this woman?* I asked myself. She was so ugly, her face twisted into that angry grimace, and her head and shoulders thrust forward as she glared. And she was armed, wielding a peanut-butter-and-jellied knife like it was Lancelot's spear!

Who is *that angry woman in the mirror?* She bore no resemblance to the kindhearted, fun-loving, patient, sweet mommy I aspired to be. Oh sure, I'd been angry, steamed, and perturbed before; I'd just never seen what it looked like. What a frightful sight, this raging maniac, this ugly witch of a woman, ready to do God knows what to innocent children! Ready to cut them—not literally but figuratively—to the quick.

I thank God today for that mirror. As I stared at my worst self, possessed by anger and out of control, I knew I needed help, because this wasn't the first time I'd gone ballistic over something trivial. It was time to do something about my anger, again. It was time to seek professional help. Again.

I went to a counselor the following Monday afternoon. The first thing she did was hand me a sheet of paper, an assessment tool that read, "Major Stressors in Life: Check all that you've experienced in the last two years." I checked. And checked. And checked some more.

The therapist, having assessed my assessment, told me, "This assessment is like a traffic light. If you checked one or two things, that's like a green light in life. 'Go ahead.' If you checked three to five things, that's like a yellow light. 'Proceed slowly, with caution.' Let's see what you checked, Mary.

"In the past two years, you've gotten divorced, remarried, and moved halfway across the country. You left all your friends and family and your entire support network. You quit one job and started a new one. You are a newlywed, a mother and stepmother, working full time outside the home and also going to school. All within the last two years!"

She paused for breath and then locked eyes with me. "The only major life change you haven't experienced in the last two years is *your own death*! This is a red light! You got here *just in time*!"

What a relief! I wasn't some crazy woman bent on peanut-buttering her children to death. I was just stressed out! That was my excuse for losing my cool and screaming my fool head off over something trivial. I was stressed out!

Yes, my feelings of anger and frustration were understandable, but—and this was the key for me—*acting out in anger was not acceptable.* My family deserved better from me. I deserved better for myself.

I needed help, again, in dealing with stress. I'd been stressed out before. I'd been angry before. I'd gotten professional help before.

Flashback

I was angry going through the breakup of my first marriage. The ending of a marriage is a long, painful, and frustrating process. In that process, my children received the brunt of my anger, pain, and frustration. I was an abusive mother.

Let me be very clear: *There is never, never, never an excuse for abusing a child—emotionally, verbally, or physically. There is never any justification, under any circumstances, to do such a thing. Ever.*

And yet I did.

I acted in anger and how I regret every destructive word, hurtful act, or abuse of trust! How I regret the tears! How I wish I could go back and undo the things I did.

How I wish I could change the past. But I can't.

God makes a promise to the Israelites through the prophet Joel: "I will repay you for the years the locusts have eaten" (Joel 2:25). Many of us who've suffered hard, painful "locust" times have appropriated that verse as God's promise to us. I realize now that I invited some of those locusts into my life myself. With angry words and actions, I brought evil down on my own house. "The wise woman builds her house, but with her own hands the foolish one tears hers down" (Proverbs 14:1). What a foolish woman I was!

Just in case you're thinking that being a Christian would have prevented the problems, or that being a Christian is the easy solution to all our troubles, think again. I was a Christian mom. I went to church. I prayed. I read the Bible. I was a "nice" person. Others told me how much they admired me for being so able — my faith being such a sustaining force — to cope with the challenges of being a single working mother to three children under seven.

But I knew the truth. The public image was one thing. What went on at our house when nobody was looking was something else entirely. The anger. The fear. The sorrow. The tears.

Those other people didn't hear me, drowning in remorse, asking my children for forgiveness. Those other people didn't hear the grace those dear little ones extended to their angry sick mother, time after time after time.

Healing comes in waves. The first wave, during that awful, angry time as a single mother, came with God's strong word. One morning, I saw the black eye I'd given one of my children the night before. As God spoke to my heart, I imagined him drawing a line across the floor. "The violence ends here. Right now. Today!" I sought professional help that very day. The violence stopped. Healing began.

Another healing wave came after the peanut-butter-and-jelly incident. God spoke to me again that day. I realized that, while my anger had been helped in the intervening years, I still needed more help in resolving the underlying issues that fueled my temper.

Oh, how blessed you are if you have never needed "outside" help to resolve the problems of your life.

How blessed you are if you have needed help, admitted it, and found it.

How sad for you, if you need help and refuse to get it. Please don't hesitate another minute. Get the help you need.

Let the healing begin.

God is in the restoration business. If you, like me, struggle with the guilt, regret, and consequences of your past actions, God longs to set you free. Will you let him begin today?

The first step to healing is to recognize that there is no excuse, no justification, for angry hurtful outbursts. There is no rationale for a bad temper. You can deal with what drives your anger later. At this moment, decide that anger will no longer control your life. Pray for God's help.

Confess your sin. Anger is an emotion; we all feel it. Feeling anger is not sin, but acting on it in hurtful ways is. "The acts of the sinful nature" include "hatred, discord, jealousy, fits of rage" among others. It's not the *feelings* of the sinful nature but the *acts* of the sinful nature that get us into trouble: "Those who live like this will not inherit the kingdom of God." (See Galatians 5:19–21.)

The good news: Jesus died for the acts of my sinful nature. He died for yours too. Confess and accept his unwarranted mercy.

Sin has consequences. God forgives the acts of our sinful nature when we confess; he promises to do so (1 John 1:9), and he keeps that promise. He will not reject a repentant heart. However, those who've been hurt by our actions are another story; we have no right to expect others to forgive us as God does. Do what's right—stop the anger and the violence—and let God take it from there. Let God guide you toward wholeness and healing.

Becoming a Christian doesn't make our problems disappear, but coming to Christ, confessing and believing, opens us up to God changing our hearts. As God's Spirit works in us, anger and frustration are replaced by tenderness and patience — not suddenly for most of us, but over time — as we continue to turn to God in trust and faith.

In time, God will change everything, if we will just let him.

Meanwhile, Back at the Ranch

As you might have guessed, I never made it down the hall that morning in California. Recovering from the shock of seeing that witch in the mirror, I hightailed it back to the kitchen, got myself a cup of coffee, and was sitting on the family room couch when the six kids came tumbling and laughing from the back bedroom. What wonderful, delightful children they were. What had I been so mad about?

"Yay! Mommy's up!" said the littlest one, snuggling next to me.

"We want to watch a movie," the oldest announced as the four in the middle plopped onto the couch and love seat, almost as one body.

"I'll get the clicker," one said, jumping up.

"I'll put in the movie," said another. Such charming children. They deserved a treat. "I'll make us some popcorn!" My suggestion was met with a unanimous cheer, which turned into a chant calling for, "Caramel corn! Caramel corn!"

With assurance from the baby that she'd save my spot, I headed to the kitchen, accompanied by the opening music of *The Neverending Story*.

It was a Brady Bunch moment.

Full Circle

In time, God will change everything, if we will just let him. My strong-willed daughter came to visit not long ago with her three-month-old son. As I looked at my beautiful girl holding her beautiful firstborn child, I felt a pang of regret for the long-ago "locust years." The pain. The anger. The sadness. I often feel that pang when I see babies. *How I wish I could have just an hour—a moment—to go back and hold my own sweet babies again, to tell them how much I love them and how sorry I am.* That regret I'll always carry.

Then I looked again at Katy and Joey and saw the tenderness in her mothering, the love in her smile as she looked down at him. "What a wonderful mother you are," I told her. "Look how relaxed and peaceful he is in your arms. He knows that you are the one who comforts him. He trusts you."

She looked at me and smiled. "I remember feeling that way in your arms too." Oh, the grace my children offer their mother! When I think back to those early days, I remember my anger and the pain. My sin has been forgiven—Jesus died for it all—and God has done a miracle in healing our family. It has taken many years, many tears, and hard, hard work. But we are healing.

What a gift my daughter gave me. Something new to remember—not that her mother was angry but that she had found comfort in my arms. What might have been a legacy of pain is being transformed, by God's generous love and unmerited grace, into a legacy of trust.

> But the fruit of the Spirit is love, joy, peace, patience, kindness, goodness, faithfulness, gentleness and self-control.
> —Galatians 5:22–23

* *

Points to Ponder

1. Have you known an angry person? What impression did they leave on you? What were the consequences of that anger?

2. Describe a time when your temper got the best of you. Bring your regret to God. Let the healing begin.

3. When, if ever, is there a time for "righteous anger"? When, if ever, is our own anger justifiable?

* *

15

The Blame Game

Did you know that "road rage" is now a medical condition? I heard it on the news this morning: that driver's fit of temper is not his or her fault, because they have a condition known as intermittent explosive disorder, or IED.

Picture this traffic stop. "Officer, I couldn't help myself! I have IED. That guy cut in front of me on the freeway, so I ran his car off the bridge." The nice police officer says, "I understand. That IED is a terrible thing to have. I'll let you off with a warning this time, as long as you promise to just simmer down, buddy. Okay?"

Or imagine this police report. "August 3rd, 7:45 a.m.: Altercation in parking lot at Shop-n-Save. Suspect is elderly female driver claiming another elderly female driver cut her off entering the parking lot, then ran ahead of her into the store and 'scarfed up' all the early bird specials. Suspect admits she slashed tires on victim's 1969 Buick Riviera. *(Note to self: Riviera in mint condition! Victim is original owner, drives only to church and Shop-n-Save. Keeps car on blocks all winter. Additional note to self: Watch obituaries.)* Suspect blames altercation on IED and states, 'Social Security check day is also senior discount day at Shop-n-Save. And this month the early bird specials were

Super PoliGrip, lemon drops, and Metamucil. She's lucky all I slashed were her tires!'"

Intermittent explosive disorder is just a fancy new name for a temper tantrum. Anger run amuck is nothing new. Every woman has had IED at one time of the month or another. Who among us hasn't lashed out in rage at a mate who has put the new toilet-paper roll on upside down? Such an affront to our delicate sensibilities deserves an angry outburst. And is there a woman alive who hasn't lashed out at a mate for the even more heinous (and no doubt more common) act of using the last of the toilet paper and not replacing the roll? Who hasn't gotten even madder realizing that, after a decade or more of living under the same roof, said mate has no clue where the extra toilet paper is stored?

Speaking of angry spouses, I'm certain Henry the Eighth suffered from IED. "Wife? Which wife? The one who died? Or the one—oops ... two—I divorced? Or the one—oops ... two—whose heads I chopped off? It wasn't my fault. I have IED and she should have known better than to put the toilet paper on upside down in the royal bathroom!" If Henry's IED and a cure had been discovered before 1533, PBS would have presented, *The One Wife of Henry VIII*. Not much of a series, but a much happier story.

Speaking of maritally induced diseases, intermittent interrupting disorder is one I've noticed in long-married couples. He starts to tell a joke and she says, "No, George, that's not the way it goes. It was two priests and a Buddhist monk."

He corrects himself, says five more words, and she interrupts again. "No, honey, it was a monkey, not a pigeon. And it was K-Mart, not Wal-Mart."

He finally says, "Well, you tell the joke, then!" to which she says, "No, dear. You're doing just fine."

Intermittent interrupting disorder is closely related to intermittent sentence finishing, and the even more serious intermittent nagging disorder, which often triggers intermittent explosive disorder in the "naggee."

Science may discover that a leading cause of IED is "I DO."

Wondering how many other famous people of the past had undiagnosed intermittent explosive disorder, I did a Google search for "mass murderers." (Imagine my surprise when this online ad popped up: "Looking for mass murderers? Find exactly what you want today on eBay"!)

My search revealed several real and fictional sufferers of intermittent explosive disorder. Jack the Ripper topped the list. If he hadn't had IED, he might have been known as Jack the Slightly Ticked Off. (Being English, he might have preferred to be called, Jack the Mildly Perturbed. Much more refined, don't you think?)

And Attila the Hun, without IED, might have been Attila the Honey. And Conan the Barbarian without IED? Conan the Teddy Bearian.

Speaking of teddy bears, Teddy Roosevelt's Rough Riders were no doubt afflicted with IED. Why else would they have run around Cuba, charging up San Juan Hill? (It's not like they were looking for Starbucks.) Without intermittent explosive disorder, Roosevelt might have led the Mosey Up San Juan Hill and his troops would be known today as the Easy Riders.

Classical literature wouldn't be the same without intermittent explosive disorder. Without IED, Mary Shelley's "monster" would have been known around the village as "that big clumsy sweetie-pie living over at Dr. Frankenstein's lab." Edgar Allan Poe's famous tale wouldn't have been about murders at all; he'd have written *Tea Time in the Rue Morgue*.

And Robert Louis Stevenson would have written *Dr. Jekyll and Mr. Rogers.*

Temper tantrums? Fits of rage? Crimes of passion? Not any more! Blame it all on intermittent explosive disorder. It's part of a trend away from taking personal responsibility and blaming all our actions on conditions or circumstances beyond our control. With a little creative thinking, we can invent a handy excuse for every problem we have.

Excuses, Excuses

For instance, I struggle with my weight, but it's not my fault. I have IBD—intermittent binge disorder—triggered by the sight of Häagen-Dazs. So there I am, drooling in the freezer section at Shop-n-Save. Store security picks up the fact that my hand is wrist-deep in what's left of a half-gallon of Cookies and Cream Light. *Shut up,* I tell my Inner Weight Watcher, *I have to sample before I buy.* (I carry a spoon at all times for just this purpose.) *Besides it's* light *ice cream, so it doesn't count!*

Store security calls in reinforcements, and suddenly the Jenny Craig Skinny Team surrounds me to do an intervention. I wail, "It's not my fault! I have intermittent binge disorder! But give me *some* credit. At least it's *light* ice cream!"

Skinny Team Leader screams in my face like a rabid drill sergeant. " 'Light' is the gateway to harder stuff! Today it's Cookies and Cream Light; tomorrow it's regular Cookies and Cream. Before you know it, you're strung out on Almond Hazelnut Swirl. Then we find you in the gutter, slurping down gallons of Rum Raisin. By then you don't just have IBD—you have IBB! Show her the future, girls!"

The other Skinny Team members surround me with full-length mirrors, forcing me out of denial. Indeed, my intermittent binge disorder has a side effect—IBB, which stands for incredibly big butt. (I guess that's a "backside effect," isn't it?)

As they strap me to a gurney and roll me out to the Fat Patrol Van, I mourn my lost loves. "Macadamia Brittle … Chocolate Peanut Butter … Crème Brulee … Dulce de Leche …"

Skinny Team Leader is alarmed. "She's starting to speak in tongues! Start an IV of Slim Fast—*stat!*"

As the cure-all drips into my system, I slip into an ice-cream induced stupor, murmuring "I have IBD … It's not my fault. It's … not … my fault."

We can blame all our troubles on a condition, or other people, or circumstances beyond our control. That way we bear no responsibility for the choices we make. We're not at fault.

We live in a no-fault world. No-fault auto insurance means nobody is really to blame for accidents; insurance companies just pay up. One time they are covering their own client's mistake, the next time it's the other guy who goofed up, but they pay anyway. It's so much cheaper than fighting things out in court.

No-fault divorce means nobody's really to blame for the failure of the marriage. No-fault divorce is touted as a kinder, gentler parting of the ways, cheaper for everyone and less traumatic for what's left of the family. Nobody is at fault. Everything works out just fine in the end, doesn't it? Doesn't it?

We live in a no-fault world, and it has been ever thus. Adam chose to bite into the apple. When God confronted him, Adam blamed Eve. "It was the woman you gave me." When God asked Eve about her part in the whole affair, she blamed the serpent.

It's not my fault. I'm not responsible. I have a condition. I was unfairly influenced. I grew up in a lousy neighborhood.

I got picked on. My sister's mother was crazy. I lost the spelling bee. I'm lonely. I have bad hair. I married a skinflint. My cousin's uncle was a monkey.

It's not my fault … not my fault … not my fault.

Financial troubles? Not my fault. It's the bank's fault for making credit too easy to get. ("Lord, it's the man you gave me. He doesn't make enough money to keep me in the lifestyle to which I'd like to become accustomed.")

Weight problem? Not my fault. I inherited IBD from my grandma. ("Lord, it's the fat gene you gave me. And you're the one who made fried chicken taste so good!")

Drinking too much? Not my fault. My father was an alcoholic. ("Lord, it's that alcoholic gene you gave me. And all the stress in my life! I need something to help me unwind, don't I?")

Marital troubles? Not my fault. He's inconsiderate. (Or she nags.) ("Lord, what happened to that sweet person I married? How could they change so much?")

Trouble with the law? Not my fault. ("Lord, as Flip Wilson used to say, 'The devil made me do it!'")

On and on it goes, this refusal to take responsibility for our actions. ("Lord, it's *your* fault. You made people this way!")

God is big on accountability and taking personal responsibility for our actions. That's what repentance is all about. Consider the case of King David in the Bible. (See 2 Samuel, chapters 11 and 12.)

To make a long story short, King David seduces a soldier's wife, while the soldier, Uriah, is on the battlefield. She gets pregnant. David tries to cover his tracks; he tries to trick Uriah into thinking the baby is his own by calling him home from battle to sleep with his wife. (This sounds like a storyline from *The Young and the Reckless*.) That plan fails because

Uriah has integrity and refuses to shirk his soldierly duty. So King David, who is sadly lacking in the integrity department at the time, arranges to have Uriah killed.

We don't have a record of it, but I can imagine David doing some blame shifting: *It's that woman's fault. She shouldn't have been on that roof looking so good. And if her husband had been at home taking care of his wife, this never would have happened. And if Uriah hadn't been such a noble character, I wouldn't have had to kill him.* Isn't that just how we are?

This is a true and tragic tale; I am not making light of it. David's wrongdoing displeased God, just as ours does. God allowed time to pass before the day of reckoning. David married the widow, and the baby was born.

But God sees all. When the prophet Nathan confronts David, the king confesses, "I have sinned against the LORD" (2 Samuel 12:13). No excuses. No blame shifting. David doesn't say, "It's not my fault," and offer excuses. With a simple acknowledgement of personal responsibility, David owns up to his actions. He has wronged the woman and her husband. He has sinned against God.

Accountability is tough. I think it's because we don't want to see ourselves as the kind of people who do the things we do. I don't want to see myself as the kind of woman who can't control her overeating. I don't want to think I'm the kind of woman who loses her temper. I don't want to see that I'm not always a sweet thoughtful wife, mother, daughter, sister, and friend.

David didn't want to see himself as an adulterer and a murderer. David didn't want to see himself as a sinner. But he was.

I don't want to see myself as a sinner either. But I am.

The good news: When we confess, God forgives. Nathan assures David, "The LORD has taken away your sin" (verse 13).

David was guilty. David confessed. David was forgiven. When we own up to our actions and confess, God promises to forgive us and to "purify us from all unrighteousness" (1 John 1:9). Our sin is no longer held against us. Jesus took care of that on the cross.

Does that mean that David and his wife lived happily ever after? No. Sin has consequences. In David's case, the baby died. Adultery, murder, idolatry, anger, jealousy, overeating, overspending, alcoholism, drug addiction, abuse, promiscuity, violence, meanness, pettiness, greed, and selfish ambition—all sin has consequences. Avoiding accountability and denying responsibility doesn't stop the consequences.

It wasn't David's confession that brought the consequences. It was David's sin. Avoiding responsibility only made things worse.

What needs confessing in your life? God knows already. Acknowledge your part. Own your actions, your choices, your decisions. Confession brings forgiveness. Forgiveness begins healing. Healing brings freedom.

Trust God to set you free—no matter what you've done—today.

Therefore, there is now no condemnation
for those who are in Christ Jesus,
because through Christ Jesus the law of the Spirit of life
set me free from the law of sin and death.
—Romans 8:1–2

Points to Ponder

1. How did you learn personal responsibility? What was the most difficult lesson for you?

2. Describe a time when you denied responsibility for your actions. Did you get away with it? Did someone else take the fall? What were the consequences of your actions? What, if anything, do you shift blame for today?

3. What did Jesus take to the cross for you? What needs confessing today? Let him take that too.

16

Traffic Jams

Our old Buick slowed to a crawl on the freeway in Los Angeles that rainy morning in December. Heading for the airport, we hit heavy traffic as we neared a road construction zone. Car after car inched forward, stopping and starting, again and again, as one by one, drivers made the slow transition through a new cloverleaf from one freeway to another. A steady morning rain made the roads slick and the construction area slimy with mud.

A stalled car in the exit lane ahead of us compounded the problem. When our turn came, we tried to maneuver around it. The Buick's rear wheels slid off the edge of the road and into a two-foot-deep puddle. *Ka-swoosh!* Water splashed up over the hood of the car. The engine died. We were stuck in the muck at the bottom of the curving on-ramp to the next freeway.

Oh no, Lord, I thought, *please not here!* I looked out the rear window. Traffic was backing up in the exit lane, drivers honking horns as if it would do some good. It never does. With the other stalled car next to us, nobody could make any progress at all.

In the back seat, three children stared at me, wide eyed. "We're stuck," I told them.

"Cool," said the boy, the oldest at twelve. He loved adventure.

"Cool," said the middle child, who loved everything her older brother loved.

"Mommy?" said the littlest one, who was six. She hated everything at the moment.

"We're stuck, and it is definitely not cool," I said, a forced calm belying—I hoped—the panic rising inside. We were in trouble. Deep stuck-in-the-muck-on-the-LA-freeway trouble.

"I'll get the car started," Terry said. "You get out and push." That's when the real trouble started.

"Excuse me?" Had the man taken complete leave of his senses?

"Get out and push," he said. "I'll drive." Had the exhaust somehow leaked into the driver's side of the car and addled his brain? I glared at him, willing him to read my thoughts. He must have.

"Well, either you get out and push, or I'll push and you can drive," he said. He was playing dirty now. He knew how much I hated freeway driving, especially in heavy traffic. And traffic didn't get any heavier than it was at that moment.

I looked back at the kids. They were waiting for my decision. The little one said, "Please, Mommy. Let Daddy drive." She'd been alone in the car with me before.

"Yeah, Mom," the oldest said. "Dad's better at it than you are." So wise at twelve. So blunt. So fearless.

"Good sports, Mom. Remember?" the middle one—the athletic one—reminded us all that good sports do what's best for the team. I was tempted to make her get out and push, but that wouldn't have been sporting.

Good sport that I am, I opened the car door. Brown greasy water lapped at the rocker panels. I've heard that everything in the world eventually ends up on the LA freeway. I believed it, looking at the debris bobbing in this puddle. A plastic Pepsi cup and fast-food bags from three different places. (What a waste. The guy who didn't finish the floating supersized fries could have traded with the guy who tossed his taco, who might have wanted the third guy's not-so-floaty filet-o-fish.)

Half a frisbee (yes, half) floated amid the carcasses of numerous insects; some of those bugs were big enough to have been playing frisbee, if they'd had a whole one. Speaking of carcasses, one was furry. A mouse? A rat? I didn't want to know. Visible through the murk were the nonfloating ingredients of this toxic stew: a disposable diaper, two beer bottles, and a tennis shoe. (Why is there always only one shoe?)

Only God knew how many wicked, flesh-eating microbes infested that nasty water, waiting for dinner. I wasn't about to be the main course. I'm just not that good a sport.

"I'm not stepping in this cesspool," I informed the family as I slammed the door closed. "That water is nasty. And it's too deep. I refuse to become the only person in history to *drown* on a freeway!" The children looked disappointed.

"Fine," Terry said, turning the key in the ignition and holding the gas pedal to the floor. The engine coughed and sputtered but failed to start. Again he tried. Again he failed.

What a helpless feeling. (This, my children, is what life was like back in the days before cell phones.) Stuck in the muck, with all the other drivers cussing us out—I knew because I'd grumbled at others a time or two myself—for making everything even worse. I could almost hear them. "Stupid idiots! Blankety blockheads! Oughta be a law! Where'd he get his driver's license—from a Wheaties box?"

Those who weren't cussing probably pitied us, which is what I do when I'm not personally inconvenienced by another driver's idiocy. "Those poor people ... tsk, tsk ... and with little children in the car. I hope someone stops to help them. I would stop to help but I have (pick one) a plane to catch / a dental appointment / shopping to do / my favorite TV show coming on in fifteen minutes. If I stop, I'll miss the flight connections / free toothbrush / big sale / season finale. Besides they look like (pick one) dangerous drug addicts waiting to rob whoever stops to help, or smart-aleck young punks who deserve car trouble for cutting everybody off and driving like maniacs."

Grumbling or tsk-tsking is so much more convenient than stopping to help.

Stuck

There we were and there was nothing we could do. Have you been there? Stuck in the muck while others move on past you, staring at you and feeling sorry for you while you remain stuck. You've tried everything. You've pushed and pushed and pushed, and still you're stuck. You're at the end of your strength, your patience, and your wits. There's nothing you can do but sit and be stuck. Your only alternative is lousy, like stepping out of the trouble into a cesspool.

Being stuck in financial troubles can feel like that. You lose your job or have your hours cut, or a medical emergency saps all your reserves. With oversized bills and downsized resources, debt piles up. You're stuck living paycheck to paycheck, trying to stay afloat while you rob Peter to pay Paul, as the saying goes. Others pass you by on the fast track to success, and you imagine them thinking, *Tsk, tsk ... those poor people, and with little children to feed. Too bad they can't get their act together.* You're thinking of bailing out of the trouble and into the cesspool of bankruptcy, despite the flesh-eating microbes of failure and shame waiting there to eat you alive.

Or maybe you're stuck emotionally, unable to move past that divorce, death, or desertion. Dreaming of the prince who'll come and awaken you with a kiss. Stuck in that imaginary fairy-tale, happily-ever-after life (the life you ordered!), waiting for rescue. Waiting to wake up from the nightmare.

Perhaps you're stuck in the past, back in the "good old days" when the children were young, or you were healthy, or life was better. And there is no alternative but stepping into the cesspool of the present, with the depressing reality of illness, loss, grief, and loneliness. Yuck.

Maybe you're stuck in the rut of routine, doing things the same way for so long you don't see that you have any alternatives. Have you not heard that insanity is doing the same thing over and over and expecting different results? You want things to be better, but you keep doing the same things over and over and you get the same results. You keep relating to that awful person the same way, expecting, hoping, that one of these days she or he will change. It never happens. It never will.

You might be stuck in the rut of habits. You wish you could stop eating too much, or be sober, or stop gambling—you want to be free, really you do!—but you can't see the way out. Sobriety—deliverance—looks like the cesspool, rife with uncertainty and teeming with the pain of admitting the problem and the hard work of recovering.

The truth is this: the real cesspool is where you are living right now, with your shameful little secret. And you are neck deep in it.

Maybe you're stuck in the muck spiritually. Is it possible? Yes. I stayed mad at God for a long time after he "took" my dad from me. *Too soon! How could God leave me fatherless at six-teen? I prayed and prayed but he died anyway. How could God allow that? I want nothing to do with that kind of God!*

Or maybe you're stuck spiritually because some fool at some church said something or did something hurtful to you or someone you cared about, and because the fool was con-nected to a church, you connected that foolishness with God. *If that's how God's people behave, then I want nothing to do with God!*

Or perhaps it was more serious than just a fool at church. Perhaps you suffered what some call spiritual abuse. Perhaps you were told you were not good enough, or didn't have faith enough, or didn't pray right, or manifest the right gifts to please God. Perhaps the gospel you heard was not the Good News at all but a "gospel" of bondage and despair, a system of striving to earn God's favor and never quite measuring up. And you ended up deciding, *If that's how God is, then I want nothing to do with God!*

Whatever it was that happened or didn't happen, you are still stuck emotionally or spiritually or whatever. Stuck. Stuck because of what someone did or didn't do. Stuck because you keep on doing what isn't working. Stuck because you invite trouble every time you say yes instead of no to that bad habit, or that addiction, or that curse you carry. Stuck because you keep listening to the lies somebody tells you, because you've listened so long you can't tell a lie from the truth anymore. So you stay stuck.

And stuck is what you are used to. Stuck starts to feel normal. Stuck is where you've lived for so long, you don't know what would happen if you got unstuck. Stepping out of stuck—letting go of the anger, or fear, or resentment—scares you. So you stay stuck. For days. Weeks. Years.

We were stuck in the muck for several long minutes that day on the freeway. Then we heard the distinctive rumble of a semi and two short blasts of its horn.

I looked out the back window, furious. I wanted to shout, "You blockhead! Stupid idiot! Can't you see we're stuck here?" Before I could speak, the sea of cars behind us had parted and the semi rolled closer to our back bumper.

You can't imagine how huge a semi truck really is until you've come face to face with its front grill. The view from the rear window was nothing but shiny steel rods over hot red metal and the word MACK.

"Yikes!" I shouted.

"Cool!" my son shouted.

I wanted to shout, "We're all gonna die!" But before I could scream, the semi made ever-so-gentle contact with our back end—*ka-chunk*—and, under semi power, we moved slowly forward. The muck sucked at our tires, reluctant to give us up. The semi continued, gently pushing us up out of the goop and back onto the terra firma of the on-ramp. Terry cranked the engine one more time and it sparked to life.

I shouted, "It's a miracle!" With happy waves of gratitude from all of us, to which the trucker blasted, "You're welcome!" on the air horn, we were on our way.

"Wow!" the oldest said as we cruised toward the airport. Wow, indeed. We talked about this Good Samaritan of the LA Freeway and the other anonymous heroes who inhabit this earth.

"I think he was an angel," the little one said, "Mack, the Angel." Of course.

"Oh, yeah?" The oldest knew better. "How did he fit in the truck with his wings?" The littlest didn't care how he did it. She was just sure that he did.

We all get stuck sometimes, stalled in our problems, our pain, or our past. Like the semi that came out of nowhere, God is the supernatural force big enough, strong enough to free us from the muck of life.

God connects with us, and if we will allow it—choose it—he pushes us, ever-so-gently, free.

> It is for freedom that Christ has set us free.
> Stand firm, then, and do not let yourselves
> be burdened again by a yoke of slavery.
> —Galatians 5:1

❋❋❋❋❋❋❋❋❋❋❋❋❋❋❋❋❋❋❋❋❋❋❋❋❋❋❋❋❋❋❋❋❋❋❋❋

Points to Ponder

1. Describe your most harrowing or exciting driving experience. What, where, when? What did the experience teach you?

2. Describe a time where you were stuck—physically, emotionally, or perhaps relationally. What helped you get unstuck?

3. Where are you stuck today? What's keeping you from moving forward? What lessons from the past might help you now? Identify three ideas for unsticking yourself. Then pray about what to do next.

❋❋❋❋❋❋❋❋❋❋❋❋❋❋❋❋❋❋❋❋❋❋❋❋❋❋❋❋❋❋❋❋❋❋❋❋

Part 3

Untwisting the Knots

Through the testing, the twisting,
the trials, and the troubles,
we learn how very real God is,
and how very much he loves us.
We stand.
We stand.

17

I Would If I Could

The warm air was tense with confrontation that April after-noon in the gymnasium at John Hay Elementary School. Two competitors—worthy opponents—eyed each other as they stood with the principal, Mrs. Able.

Cindy and I were facing off, each vying for bragging rights as Best Speller in the Sixth Grade. I'd won the classroom title in the preliminary rounds in Mr. Renard's class. Cindy had taken top honors in the other sixth-grade classroom.

And now here we stood, two accomplished, fast-spelling word-slingers, ready to shoot it out for the school champion-ship. The winner would go on to compete against spellers across the city, and from there, who knew? The state? The nationals? *Oh, the thought! My mother would be crying, my father beaming as I out-spelled kids from all over the country.* Mrs. Able's sharp, "Ahem!" burst my bubble.

I squinted at Cindy, giving her the evil eye. She squinted back, curling her upper lip. Wordfight at the Sixth Grade Cor-ral. Only one of us would be standing at the end of the after-noon, and we both knew it.

Our rivalry began the year before, when we were in the same fifth-grade classroom. Cindy was smart. So was I. But

Cindy was also bubbly, perky, spunky, twinkly, sparkly, funny, cute, sweet, and every other synonym for adorable.

And I was, well, smart.

But smart had paid off for me thus far in my long and illustrious elementary-school career. Smart had won me approval from teachers in the past, and so, from the first day of fifth grade, I quietly competed with Cindy for the attention of Mr. Benson, our adorable young teacher. (Male teachers were rare in the elementary schools. To have a male teacher, and a gorgeous hunk at that, was almost too much for our prepubescent psyches to bear. That there was a Mrs. Benson somewhere out there was irrelevant.) Each day I raced to hand in my work before Cindy. I went into overdrive to get higher test scores. But Cindy met the challenge every time; in fact, she always seemed to be one step ahead of me.

The boys loved her. She was Veronica; I was Betty. The girls admired her. She was Marcia; I was Jan. She was the life of the fifth-grade party. She was Lucy; I was Ethel. And I could barely tolerate it.

Later that year, we learned that the Bensons would soon have their first baby. The class divided along traditional gender lines: the boys couldn't have cared less, while the girls obsessed over the news. The playground was abuzz. Which would be better—a boy or girl? A girl, of course. What do you think they'll name it? I don't know if every girl in the class hoped to have the baby named after her, but I certainly did. Mary Benson. It had a nice ring. And Mary was "a grand old name," as my father sang. And it was Jesus' mom's name, for heaven's sake! What more could a kid want?

The day came when Mr. Benson made the big announcement. The baby was born. "It's a girl." Groans from the boys; giggles from the girls. "And we've named her ..." He paused while the distaff half of the class sucked in its collective breath. "Cindy."

Cindy. She beamed. She knew and I knew that she'd won a victory so huge nobody could touch her. Cindy, Cindy, Cindy. The class applauded. Everybody was happy. Everybody but me. It was obvious that Mr. Benson loved Cindy, so the boys couldn't help but adore her. The other girls squealed their admiration as Cindy sat there basking in the certainty of her legacy. The Queen of the Class. Teacher's Pet to End All Pets. The Girl They Named the Baby After.

Cindy had it all. And I was nothing. A big fat nothing. Nada. Zero. Zip. Zilch.

I don't know what life was like for Baby Cindy Benson, Teacher's Child, but I consoled myself the rest of fifth grade that she would one day go to her mother in tears and ask, "Why, oh why, did you have to name me Cindy? Why couldn't you name me Laura or Jenny or Katy or Betsy? Or Ethel or Gertrude or Elsie—*any*thing but Cindy! I hate that name!" Her mother would hug her daughter and say, "I'm so sorry sweetheart, but it was your father's idea. I wanted to name you Mary, after Jesus' mom. It is, after all, such a grand old name."

And now here we were a year later, Cindy and I, facing each other. This was the High Noon of Spelling. The principal fired the first word. Cindy nailed it. She was fast, no question. I returned fire with a correct spelling of my own.

Back and forth we went, each one spelling for all she was worth. The minutes ticked by. Is there anything louder than a big old school clock ticking behind its wire cage in a silent gymnasium? (Yes, children, clocks used to actually tick.) On and on we spelled, I with palms sweating, face burning, and heart thumping. The gym was getting smaller, the air thicker.

It was harder and harder to breathe. Sweat ran down the middle of my back. Cindy looked as cool as always.

Round after round, we stood our ground. Word by word, we endured. The words got tougher. Would the next bring victory or defeat?

Mrs. Able turned toward me. "Assessment," she said. My word. *Huh?* I'd never heard the word and had no clue what it meant. I took a guess.

"A-S-E-S-S-M-E-N-T?" In retrospect, a pretty good guess. Mrs. Able smiled her regret as she shook her head. The vultures started circling. I sensed the lights dimming, like when a dark cloud passes in front of the sun. Or when a criminal gets the chair. Our inquisitor turned to Cindy. My only hope was that the enemy was as clueless as I was.

But when had Cindy ever been clueless? She smiled — more a smirk, it seemed — at me, confident. She beamed the same beam she'd beamed that awful day back in Mr. Benson's class. I imagined her mocking me, "Nyah, nyah, nyah, nyah, nyah, nyah ... They named the baby after me ... Now I'm gonna win the spelling bee ... and yer-er nah-aht." Kids can be so mean.

Cindy smiled at Mrs. Able. "Assessment. A-S-S-E-S-S-M-E-N-T. Assessment." Mrs. Able smiled. Cindy smiled back exultant. The rest of the showdown is a blur. Cindy spelled a final word correctly — I have no recollection of what the word was; my ears were ringing too loudly for me to hear — and clinched the title. She beamed bigger than ever. Everybody was happy. Everybody but me. My cheeks burned hotter as tears stung my eyelids. I thought I might pass out or, worse, start blubbering right there in front of the principal or, worse still, Cindy. (I blubbered all the way home later instead.)

I don't remember congratulating Cindy. If I did, it was the last civil word we exchanged until high school. I'm embarrassed to admit it, but I boiled with envy toward Cindy all through junior high. The in-crowd blessed her with popularity. Her parents blessed her with a better wardrobe than I had. Puberty blessed her with bigger boobs.

And I was pathetic, making jokes at her expense and belittling her behind her back every chance I had. But the more I hated Cindy, the worse I felt. Envy is a nasty thing. That "green-eyed monster" is indeed a monster, devouring us.

No question about it: losing stinks, even if it's not whether you win or lose but how you play the game. Whatever. You and I both know it feels better to win. But the worst of it wasn't losing to Cindy. The worst of it was the effect that loss had on my attitude.

Chain Reaction

That loss triggered a chain reaction that became a pattern well into my adult life. Losing made me afraid of losing again. Failing so publicly made me afraid to fail again. I didn't have the confidence, the strong sense of self-worth to take another risk like that. My sense of self-worth depended on my performance and the approval of others. I had failed to perform. I had failed to be approved. I wasn't going to take the chance of it happening again. Not if I could help it.

Call it a case of arrested development. As I grew older, given the choice between hard and easy, I took the easy way. When offered a new challenge, if I couldn't guarantee that I would win, I wouldn't even try. If I couldn't be perfect at something, I wouldn't attempt it. Given a choice, I opted for those things that came easiest to me.

I avoided anything challenging, anything outside my comfort zone. If I thought I was going to lose in a situation—a new relationship, a sports challenge, a job promotion—I avoided the situation. I didn't enter into contests I couldn't win. I settled for mediocre jobs in which I could easily excel. I gravitated toward relationships that were predictable. I avoided people and situations that might force me out of that comfort zone. Each time I drew back from a challenge, it made it easier to draw back the next time. This was my attitude: I would if I could but I can't guarantee success, so I won't try. (*I'd apply to that college, but they might say no. I'd put in for that promotion, but I might not get it.*)

I would if I could but I can't be certain of what it would mean. (*I'd leave this awful relationship, or kick this addiction, or stop this behavior, or let go of the past ... but then what? What would happen next? Who will I be?*)

I would if I could but I can't be the best, so I won't even attempt it. (*I'd sign up for that piano recital, but I might make a mistake in public. I'd enroll in that night school class, but Cindy might be in there.*)

In other words, I played it safe.

What is God's "assessment" of that kind of life? A playing-it-safe life is only half a life. It's a life without challenge, life without risk. Life without life. Do you know people who never take a chance, never reach for a dream, never risk anything for fear of failure? Do you know people who play it safe, who live as if their only goal is to get safely to death?

Are you one of them? I certainly have been.

We are not here to be safe. We are here to do what God has called us to do. We are here to do the difficult, the uncomfortable, the challenging, and sometimes the "impossible." To bear the unbearable, to love the unlovable, to confront evil, and to trust God when all seems hopeless.

We are here to dash ourselves against the rocks, swim against the current, fall in love, and have our hearts broken. We are here to live!

The Bible is full of stories of passionate living, of suffering, and of sacrifice. I don't know about your experience, but I've found that what God has called me to do in this life is hardly ever within my comfort zone. He asks me to do hard things—to take chances and risk rejection. To go ahead and love, risking that I might not be loved back. To go ahead and forgive, even when nobody said they were sorry. To go ahead and attempt what seems impossible. To go ahead and jump off the cliff of life and trust that he will provide the net, or the wings!

I'm trusting God to help me change that losing pattern of my life. As time goes on, experience accumulates. Sometimes I risk and flop. Sometimes risk rewards me. Sometimes imperfection turns out to be just, well, perfect. Or at least good enough.

But old habits, and old hurts, die hard. To this day, the word *assessment* conjures up Cindy's smirk. I discovered after the spelling showdown that our local paper had published a huge list of spelling bee practice words, including *assessment*. Cindy had practiced. I had not. She won. I lost. Simple as that.

And my losing was probably for the best, I decided much— much—later. The national winner that year was a boy named John from Tulsa. The winning word was *smaragdine*. I'd never heard the word *assessment*; what chance would I have had with *smaragdine*? I looked it up; *smaragdine* has something to do with emeralds. Smaragd is my birthstone. Oh, the irony.

(The following year's winning word was even worse: *esquamulose*, which means—just in case you're curious and don't have quick access to Google—"not squamulose." Anyone who knew that might benefit from the 1940 winner: *therapy*.)

Yes, old habits die hard. As I'm writing this, a niggling thought in the back of my mind conjures old fears. You see, if I finish this book, I'll have to send it to my editor. She might not like it. There is a strong possibility—very strong, given past experience—that I will be rewriting parts of it. The book won't be perfect, even though I'll be submitting the umpteenth revision.

So do I say, "I'd finish the book but I can't because it won't be perfect"? No, because time and experience have taught me that it can't be, and doesn't have to be, perfect. It just has to be the best book it can be. And if it is, then it will be accepted and printed and "out there."

But then what? I could say, "I can't finish the book because once it gets out there, someone might hate it." The fact is someone out there is *sure* to hate it. What is my fear, really? "I'd finish this book if I could, but I can't be positive that everyone who reads it will love it, and by extension, love me"? Those niggling thoughts can be rather ridiculous. Those thoughts can keep us stuck in the half-life of mediocrity.

But we all have them. Fill in your own blanks today. "I would _____ if I could, but I can't because _____." What's got you stuck? Have you a project or a dream you haven't dared to try because you tried and failed before? Have you stayed far too long in a job you hate, just because you don't know what will come next? Have you stayed far too long in a destructive relationship, just because you don't know what will happen if you end it? Have you stayed far too long than was healthy with a habit that was killing you, just because you couldn't imagine life without it?

You don't have to be stuck. You have options. Don't let those niggling thoughts, those what-if fears, run your life. God has a better way to live.

It's obvious that I did finish the book. It turned out that I could finish it after all. And as you are reading this, I'm on to the next project. (I don't know what it is today, but by the time you read this I'll have figured it out.) You don't have to be stuck. You don't have to stay with that job, or that relationship, or that bad habit. You don't have to fear the future. You can move forward the same way I finished this book. Step by step. Moment by moment. Day by day. Trusting God.

It's time to stop saying, "I would if I could but I can't." It's time to say "I can." It's time to trust. Will you?

> I press on to take hold of that
> for which Christ Jesus took hold of me. . . .
> Forgetting what is behind and straining toward what is ahead,
> I press on toward the goal to win the prize
> for which God has called me heavenward in Christ Jesus.
> —Philippians 3:12–14

* *

Points to Ponder

1. Chicken Little or Mighty Mouse? Which are you most often, and how so? What is the bravest thing you ever did? What gave you the courage to do it?

2. Recall a time when you lost. What did you lose? (A prize, a relationship, your confidence?) What did you gain? How has your perspective changed over time?

3. Think of a dream, a project, or a goal you've been putting off, for whatever reason. Fill in the blank: "I would

   _____ if I could, but I can't

   because _____."

   Now rewrite it: "If I trusted God for (with) _____

   _____, he might _____

   _____ and I might

   _____."

   What is your next step? When will you take it?

* *

18

Wedding Whine

Early June. Our dining room looks like a bride exploded in it. White tulle—yards and yards of it—is heaped on the table. A dozen giant tulle bows hang like fluffy white butterflies from a wooden curtain rod extended between two of the dining room chairs. Twelve bows down, a hundred to go. Making tulle bows to decorate the church and reception hall is just one of the gazillion things on my mother-of-the-bride to-do list.

The Strong Willed Child's late June wedding had been a year in the planning. The invitations, the ceremony, the music, the reception, the dinner, and a million little details are finally coming together for this elegant, God-honoring celebration of the joy of new love.

But there is no joy in Momville. I'm steaming mad.

Flash back to New Year's Day. My stepson calls from Los Angeles with big news: he's engaged. *We'll have another wedding in the family! How delightful!*

Mid-January. He calls to say that he and his fiancée have started planning. They'll be married in a small intimate ceremony in LA, at sunset, overlooking the ocean. *How romantic! Of course, we'll be there!*

The date? Late June. Six days before his stepsister's wedding in Wisconsin.

Excuse me?

February, March, April, May. I fume. I know, I know—I should have been delighted that we'd be blessed with two weddings in the family. And I was, really I was. I should have been thrilled that another one of our children had found love. And I was, really, I was. I should have been a grown-up about the whole thing, but I wasn't. Really. I wasn't.

You see, I hadn't planned to add "Make a cross-country trip six days before the wedding" to my mother-of-the-bride to-do list. Being "forced" to do so made me angry. Really angry. And I have the journal pages to prove it. Here are some excerpts:

Sometime in February: "Their timing stinks! I just don't understand how they can be so selfish. I need to pray about this because right now I've got resentment and harshness building up that I know is not pleasing God. But I am really, really upset, and I feel guilty about being so upset. I shouldn't be upset. I should be loving and Christian and forgiving and accommodating. But this is eating me *up* ..."

A few weeks later: "Up at 4:00 a.m. and this wedding thing is just stuck in my craw and I cannot let it go. I could just stay home and pout. Or stay home and pretend I'm making a statement about what is right and fair and decent. Or I could go because Terry will make me miserable if I don't. Or go and act like a complete jerk. Or go and just pretend that everything is wonderful. Go and pretend? What would Dr. Phil say? What would Dr. Laura recommend? Go and pretend, no doubt. I just don't know if I can pull that off.

"God, I'm scared to fly with all the terrorist stuff going on. What if something happens to us? What if there's an earthquake while we're there? What if we can't get back? I'm scared and miserable about the whole thing. I hate that I have to go and *give* when I don't want to *give*! I hate that I *have* to go and be nice when I'm *hurt*! And hurt feelings are what this is about and I have them and *nobody* seems to care about *my* feelings ... Help me Jesus!"

(Sheesh! You're probably not as melodramatic as I am. It's embarrassing to let you see what goes on in my brain, but I hope you feel better now about your own thoughts.)

It helps to talk to someone about your feelings, doesn't it? I tried to talk to my sweet husband about the way his son was making me feel. Here's the journaled recap: "I just told Terry again exactly what I felt about the wedding plans, and he said, 'Just don't have that feeling! *Get over it!*' Can you imagine that? He said, '*Just forget about it!*' So I said, 'I *will* forget it! I'm not going to the wedding. *I am not going.* There! *That* is *that!*'"

My dear husband and I had a terrible fight that day. He didn't understand my feelings. And he was so defensive! (Maybe because I kept saying, "*Your* son ..."? What do you think?) So we ended up screaming at each other.

That wasn't like us. Terry and I had been parenting our blended crew for nearly twenty years. We'd refused from the beginning to get caught up in that "your kids, my kids" kind of nonsense. We'd seen the destruction that causes when you're trying to rebuild a family.

When people asked how we'd managed to keep relative harmony among the six children, we joked, "We decided early to ignore them all equally." Just a joke, but with a ring of truth; we'd tried to deal evenhandedly with all the children. But we'd never faced this kind of uneven situation.

And the wedding situation wasn't the only thing on my mind that spring. Life had become a twisted mess. In the middle of planning the wedding, I was working to finish my second book. (*Will I finish by the deadline?*) I lost a regular writing job. (*Will I be able to replace that income?*) Two of my closest friends moved out of state; another took a new job requiring extensive travel. (*Will I have any friends left?*)

Terry developed glaucoma. (*Will he go blind?*) The youngest daughter was caught in a late spring blizzard while traveling. (*Will she make it home safely?*) She also announced she'd be moving back home—again—after the college semester ended. (*Will she ever leave?*) Another daughter had a miscarriage. (*Will she be able to have more children?*) A close relative lost his job and was temporarily homeless. (*Will he find another job? Another home?*) Two other close relatives passed away. (*Will the sadness ever end?*)

My mother was getting more and more forgetful. (*Is it Alzheimer's?*) My dearest childhood friend was battling cancer. (*Will she survive?*) The nation was at war. (*Will any of us survive?*)

And oh yeah, I was in the throes of menopause. (*Will I ... Can I ... Where was I? Oh well, whatever.*)

All of this happened within a terrible six-month period. I whined and complained to my few remaining friends. (I ignored the feeling that perhaps those other two had moved so they wouldn't have to listen to me whine and complain.) My friends—bless them—listened, commiserated, and promised to pray for me. And I wrote in my journal.

Too many changes and challenges in too short a time. Not enough time to absorb one thing before another thing happens. The feeling that life is dumping on you and everything is out of control. You can't think. You can't breathe.

Have you been there? If so, you know that planning a wedding is *enough* to deal with. A death in the family, friends leaving, worries about children—any one of those is enough to deal with. To deal with several at once is overwhelming.

Journaling about my feelings helped. It was while journaling one morning that God helped me to see the heart of the issue as I thought and wrote about my stepson's wedding plans: "I've been a stepmother for almost twenty years, and this is the first time any of the kids has made me feel like I don't matter or like we're not a family."

"Like we're not a family"? Ridiculous. We *were* a family. Blended and bonded together by time and love, if not blood. A family. Period.

"Like I don't matter"? Ah, there it was. How much of it was about *me* and *my* feelings and *my* hurt? Did I really want—as a mother—to have adult children making their decisions based on how they might affect me, me, *me*? Absolutely not! Ridiculous. Period.

God opened my eyes to my self-absorption. Writing about it helped me to see the truth, that self-absorption is what bred my anger, hurt, frustration, and rebellion. Self-absorption, and the evil it breeds, is a spiritual matter. Every frustration, every sorrow, every angry outburst comes down to a spiritual matter, a matter of our relationship with the Lord. Here's an example from my journal that May; my inner strong-willed child speaks loud and clear: "I am rebelling right now against going to that wedding. I know what's right. I know what I should do. *But I don't want to do what's right!* It's a *spiritual matter*. I'm not in control of this situation, and I don't like that. I want things my way."

It seems that every difficult situation boils down to a spiritual issue. At least it does for me. At the core of the problem, if I'm willing to look into my own heart, I'll see the real issue. Rebellion. Pride. Greed. Lust. Anger. In other words: sin.

The source of my anger, resentment, and hurt, the source of my stress and frustration in the wedding situation, was my unwillingness to acknowledge that God is in control. We don't have control, but only the occasional illusion of control. Or perhaps it is a *delusion* of control. Our ability to manipulate others into doing things our way isn't really control, is it? We may be able to influence events, but our influence depends on the other people involved being willing to go along with our desires.

When it comes to control, only God truly has it. Only God has willpower—the power to exert his will over circumstances. The best we can do is try to keep up with him, to go where he is going, to follow where he is leading. When we decide not to do that, when we dig in our heels and demand to have things our way instead of his, the spiritual battle begins.

My stubborn refusal to pray, my stubborn angry refusal to release the situation to God, to be open to what God might want—all of that was tearing me apart. All of that was causing pain and stress among those I love the most.

We were on the brink of disaster, just as surely as if I'd added "Destroy everything with my nasty attitude" to my mother-of-the-bride and stepmother-of-the-groom to-do lists.

As I prayed and thought and journaled and talked some more, I began to see that I was asking the wrong questions. In fact, I'd been asking a lot of the wrong questions for a long time. Questions like, Why me? Why this? Why my husband? Why my friend? Why my mother? Why now? Why is there menopause?

All are futile questions, with useless answers. Why not you? Why not this? Why not him, or her, or them? The ultimate answer God could deliver, like a mother telling her child, "Because I'm the Mommy, that's why!"

When I started asking better questions, I began to find better answers. Is there an issue you've been wrestling with? Is there a rocky relationship, a bad habit, or a change you've been struggling with?

"Why?" is a dead end. Better questions—asking who, what, where, when, and how can I—those questions start us on the path to better answers.

> We will not hide these truths from our children;
> we will tell the next generation
> about the glorious deeds of the LORD,
> about his power and his mighty wonders.
> —Psalm 78:4 NLT

✳✳✳

Points to Ponder

1. Have you ever planned a wedding? Describe a wedding disaster you've been involved in. Describe the perfect wedding.

2. Is it possible for parents to love all their children equally? Why or why not? Is there a difference between loving all "the same" and loving all "equally"? If so, how so?

3. What is your greatest challenge in loving others as God loves you (consistently, unconditionally)? Who do you find unlovable or have difficulty loving? Pray about this.

✳✳✳

19

Better Questions.
Better Answers

When bad stuff happens, we ask, Why me? Why this? Why now? We ask, but those questions don't have any good answers.

"Just because" certainly isn't a good answer; it throws us into the fog of fate, a universe of randomness. "Just because ..." what? That's life? That's the way the cookie crumbles? It was in the stars?

Or if God is involved, then why? Just because God is mean? Or God is not in control? Or maybe just because God doesn't love you, or he's out to get you? If you could know the reason why, would it make any difference? Would it make the bad thing go away?

"Why me?" might be the normal response as we grieve, but moaning and groaning, fussing and complaining—all the "why-ning" in the world—won't get you any closer to a resolution of the problem. Whine long enough and you'll develop a victim mindset, a pattern of persecution and all-or-nothing thinking that leads nowhere. *Why does bad stuff always happen to me? Why am I always the one the universe decides to pick on? Why does everyone always dump on me?*

Do you hear the paranoia? Do you hear the self-absorption? Asking better questions will lead to better answers.

You've lived life. You've survived the twists and troubles of the past. I'd like to offer you a pattern for thinking, a pattern that you've probably followed in one way or another without even being aware of it, many times before, as you've dealt with the challenges of your life. Here is my version, a method of purposeful thinking that will help you tap into your immense store of experience and knowledge hard-earned in life's school of hard knocks. This is a method of asking better questions, the kind of questions that will help you find the answers you already know and open your mind and heart to options you might not have realized are available to you.

Let's get started. What's on your heart and mind right now? What issue has you twisted in a knot? Is it a rocky relationship? Is it a bad habit that you just can't seem to kick? Is it one of those major stresses that we all experience? Is it a sudden and devastating change of your life's course — a disappointment, a diagnosis, or a death? What has hold of your heart and mind right now?

Using my own example from the previous chapter, here is a technique for working through the big stuff of life. (I know what you're thinking: *Oh no! I thought she'd be done whining about that wedding thing by now.* Stay with me here; there's hope.) At the end of this chapter you'll find these questions in worksheet form. Feel free to make copies for your own use.

(1) Simplify. In *five* words or less, the issue I'm struggling with is …

What? Five words or less? But you don't understand! My issue is so huge, so complex and has been going on for soooo long.

Why so few words? We magnify our tale of woe as we tell the tale to others. My stories tend to grow and grow as I tell them over and over again. With each friend's expression of support, I embellish things a little more. I'm not exactly lying; I'm just exploring the truth.

What started out as a painful but relatively simple issue expands in the telling. Soon it has taken on a gargantuan dimension in my life. It's become the worst thing that anyone living on the earth has ever had to deal with! It must be, if all my friends feel so bad about it!

I'm an expert at making mountains out of molehills. The discipline of forcing myself to condense the big story down to the one critical point helps me clear away the extraneous feelings and get started toward resolution. We can't solve a dozen problems at once. But one at a time, we can deal with them. Stating the issue in as few words as possible will focus your efforts.

Here are my five words: I am resentful about the wedding. (Okay, that's six. Close enough.)

(2) What I need to know is ... (Ask *ten* questions about the issue. Resist asking "why?")

Ask questions that start with what, where, when, who, and how. What can I do? Where can I look, or go, for help? When will I start? Who can help me figure this out? How can I get over this, past this, through this?

You are not expecting any answers, or even great questions, at this point. You are just expressing questions that take you out of the "why" zone.

"How can I" questions are the most helpful. But beware; asking "How can they/he/she?" is another dead end. It's just that "why-victim" mentality in disguise. How can they be so selfish? How can she be so insensitive? How can he do this to me? These questions get you nowhere.

Here are my questions: What is making me feel this way? What do others in the family think? What are my options? Who can I talk to? How can I deal with this? How can I find peace? How can I see this from their point of view?

When will I get over it? (This is a great question, because it opens my mind and heart to the idea that I *will* get through it.) What does God have to say about this? How can I honor God in this situation? (This may be the best question of all.)

Just asking questions at this point, without seeking answers, clears the issue in your thoughts. Just asking questions gets you started toward resolution.

(3) Control: I can control … I cannot control …

Have you realized by now that you cannot control other people? You cannot force them to make decisions based on what you think is best. (*But oh, how much simpler life would be for all of us if everyone would just do what I wanted them to do.*)

The answer to the first part of this question is simple. The only thing I can control in any situation: my atti-toot!

We cannot control other people. We cannot control the fact of disease, war, famine, or death. The list of what we cannot control is so much longer than the list of what we can control.

My answer to the second part of this question: I have no control over the date they set, which is the same date as her grandmother's birthday, and she wanted to honor her grandmother. I cannot control my husband's feelings. I cannot change the fact of this wedding date. Period.

(4) The worst possible and best possible outcomes would be …

Usually imagining the worst is a waste of time and energy. But in this case, we are imagining the worst outcome based on our worst behavior. For example, if I learned I had six months to live, the worst-case scenario might be that I would spend those six months getting back at all the people who've ever hurt me. Or spend that time accumulating debt I know I'll never pay back. Or letting the diagnosis of my illness compromise my values and ruin the remaining days of my life. Or wasting my last days whining.

As I thought through this question, I imagined at first that the worst possible outcome would be that Terry and I would die in a fiery plane crash. The children would be heartbroken, of course. But we'd be in heaven; would that be the worst thing?

Eventually I realized what the worst outcome really was. The worst-case scenario would be hurting and alienating my children and my sweet husband. I didn't want that to happen.

Once we've imagined the worst-case scenario, it's time to dream the dream: What would the best-case scenario be? This helps us to see a future different from the current situation. This kind of imagining will focus our efforts. Imagining the best outcome helps build optimism and hope. We might be able to get through this after all.

My answer to this one: The best possible outcome would be that we go and have a great time, and there are no problems with this. And everyone lives happily ever after! (Wow. There it is again—the life I ordered!)

(5) Things I've tried that have not helped the situation and attitudes of mine that might have gotten in the way ...

Sometimes, in trying to force a solution, we get in the way of a solution. Now it is true-confession time. In dealing with your challenging situation, have you done anything so far that has been less than helpful? In thinking this one through, we open our minds to the possibility that maybe, just maybe, we might be doing things that make matters worse. If we're honest about it.

Based on the journal entries of the previous chapter, you can probably figure out my answer: scream, pout, demand, be rude, snarl, whine about it to everyone who would listen, and in general, act like a complete jerk.

Yep. I'd been getting in the way.

We're open here to the possibility that maybe, just maybe, we might need an attitude adjustment. Maybe. Fear, anger, resentment, entitlement, envy—all are attitudes that can get in the way.

In my situation, I identified a couple of less-than-helpful attitudes. First was the "*My* versus *your* mentality" involving our children. Somehow the blessing of two weddings in the family became an emotional battle over *my* daughter's wedding versus *his* son's wedding. Resentment was the second attitude that made my list; not just feeling resentment, but holding on to it, letting it fester, and letting it spew out in anger. Maybe, just maybe, I did need that adjustment.

(6) What does God say about this? What would Jesus do?

Here is where we discover that God has something to say about every issue we deal with. Check the topical index in your Bible for specific verses, or consult a Bible-studying friend for suggestions.

In my case, God had plenty to say: "Rejoice in the Lord always. I will say it again: Rejoice! Let your gentleness be evident to all. The Lord is near. Do not be anxious about anything, but in everything, by prayer and petition, with thanksgiving, present your requests to God. And the peace of God, which transcends all understanding, will guard your hearts and your minds in Christ Jesus. Finally, brothers, whatever is true, whatever is noble, whatever is right, whatever is pure, whatever is lovely, whatever is admirable—if anything is excellent or praiseworthy—think about such things" (Philippians 4:4–8).

And this: "Whatever happens, conduct yourselves in a manner worthy of the gospel of Christ" (Philippians 1:27).

And this: "If you claim to be religious but don't control your tongue, you are just fooling yourself, and your religion is worthless" (James 1:26 NLT). (This last one comes up often as I wrestle in life; do you think maybe God is trying to tell me something?)

What would Jesus do? This is the toughest question in some cases, for Jesus didn't do what was easy. I don't see any evidence that Jesus ever responded by screaming, pouting, demanding, being rude, snarling, or whining about his issues to everyone who would listen. I find no evidence that Jesus ever acted like a jerk. Jesus loved, had compassion, forgave, understood, and comforted. Jesus stayed focused on his mission: to bring glory to God by doing what he was here on earth to do. "I have brought you glory on earth by completing the work you gave me to do. And now, Father, glorify me in your presence with the glory I had with you before the world began" (John 17:4–5). Jesus also said, "Do to others as you would have them do to you" (Luke 6:31).

My answer: Jesus would model the Golden Rule and make his love and compassion known to all, that God might be glorified through this.

(7) Other resources that might help with this issue are ... (friends, books, professional advice)

Open your mind and heart to support from others, via books, websites, groups, or one-on-one contact with caring trustworthy friends and professional counselors. You don't need to go it alone. Help is out there!

My resources: prayer, trusted friends, wedding etiquette books (not so that I could get backup to support my position but for ideas on handling myself in a gracious manner), and my own loving heart. (I do have one, really I do. I counted it as a resource, trusting that maybe, just maybe, my love for the children would prevail.)

(8) My prayer is ...

Open your heart to pray about the issue. Tell God all about it. Let him lead you toward his solution.

My prayer began: "Lord, help me to come to terms with and to be at peace with this fact of my life."

(9) One thing I hadn't thought of before is ...

Praying and thinking through an issue gives us new insight. What-if thinking is powerful. Make note of that one thing you hadn't thought of before. And make note also of any other new ideas that come your way.

My answer: We just might go and have a wonderful time. God just might use us to share his love with all involved. This might be a good thing for me, to have this chance to travel and take a little break from all the wedding plans here.

(10) My next step will be ...

You've prayed. You've thought. You've wrestled with this issue. Do you sense a next step to take? Perhaps you've come up with a list of options; write them down, and then pray and think some more to identify the next step.

My next step was: go and smile.

Epilogue

Journal entry for July 15: "The weddings are done. Both were beautiful. Danny got married at the beach in California. I didn't want to go, but the Lord spoke clearly to me through the Word: 'Whatever happens, conduct yourselves in a manner worthy of the gospel of Christ,' and, 'Let your gentleness be evident to all.' I love it when he speaks so precisely for the situation.

"So I went. While I watched the bride and groom, I realized that Dan is all grown up now, and he is so much like his father—a sweet man who wants the woman he loves to be happy. And the trip turned out to be a wonderful break from the wedding craziness here. Who knew? God, of course. As usual.

"Thanks, Lord. Again."

> Trust in the LORD with all your heart;
> do not depend on your own understanding.
> Seek his will in all you do,
> and he will show you which path to take.
> **—Proverbs 3:5–6 NLT**

❋❋❋❋❋❋❋❋❋❋❋❋❋❋❋❋❋❋❋❋❋❋❋❋❋❋❋❋❋❋❋❋❋❋❋❋❋

Points to Ponder

Now it's your turn. On the following page, you will find the Life Issues Worksheet. Feel free to make copies for your own use in working through the issues of your life. May God bless you in the process!

❋❋❋❋❋❋❋❋❋❋❋❋❋❋❋❋❋❋❋❋❋❋❋❋❋❋❋❋❋❋❋❋❋❋❋❋❋

Life Issues Worksheet

1. In *five* words or less, the issue I'm struggling with is:

2. What I need to know is: (Ask ten questions about the issue. Ask "What ... Who ... Where ... When ..." and especially "How can I ...")

3. In this situation, I can control:

   In this situation, I cannot control:

4. Worst possible outcome:

   Best possible outcome:

5. Things I've tried / attitudes of mine that haven't helped the situation:

6. What does God say (Scripture)? What would Jesus do?

7. Other resources that might help me with this issue (books, professional advice, friends):

8. My prayer is:

9. One thing I hadn't thought of before is:

10. My next step will be:

20

My Toy Is Missing

It was a warm June noon when Grandpa Terry and I took two of our grandchildren to lunch at the mall food court. Justin, who was six, and his sister Megan, almost three, were visiting Wisconsin from California with their parents; this was a rare opportunity for some intergenerational bonding.

Megan and I went to a pizza counter, where she got a piece of pizza, a cup of milk, and a small bag of cookies shaped like little teddy bears. Megan was calmly eating her pizza when Justin and Grandpa came to the table. They'd been to a hamburger chain and Justin had one of their kids' meals.

Justin ignored his burger and held up a little clear-plastic bag, carefully examining the toy inside. He glanced at his sister, who regarded this with keen, little-sisterly interest. He began to slowly, painstakingly, unwrap the toy, savoring, I'm sure, the big-brotherly power he wielded. Megan watched, enthralled.

This was not just any old toy. This toy was special. This was a spinning wonder, a gyroscopic, superhero dream of a toy. Justin gave it a spin and it whirled across the tabletop. Both children watched, wide eyed.

After several spins of the toy, Justin finally unwrapped his burger and took a bite. He spun the toy again, watching as he chewed and swallowed. He took another bite and gave the toy another spin. He continued to spin it, as big brothers will do, in such a position that his little sister could see it but not touch it. He knew she wanted to. We all knew. He leaned forward slightly to shield it, partially, so that she had to lean forward to see it.

Kids! I waited for the fireworks to start. Megan frowned, looking down at her lunch. She looked at the toy, looked at her lunch tray, looked back at the toy, and then looked up at me, brown eyes wide, and said, matter-of-factly, "My toy is missing."

If you know children, you are probably thinking what I was thinking in that moment. *Uh-oh, here it comes! The whining. The fighting. The screaming.* I knew I had to defuse the bomb before it exploded. I had to make lemonade out of Megan's lemons. I had to give the girl some reason to go on living, so I said, "Yes, Justin has a toy, but *you* get to have teddy-bear cookies. That's like having a toy, but *you* get to eat them!"

Not bad for a decrepit old granny, I thought. Megan regarded me darkly and skeptically. Would she buy it? I waited as she mulled my suggestion.

And then, in what may be the most miraculous moment in child-rearing history I'll ever have the privilege to witness, Megan shrugged her shoulders, gave me a little smile, grabbed a teddy-bear cookie and popped it in her mouth. She never mentioned her brother's toy again.

Wow. No screaming. No whining. No fighting. How could it be? Was it her personality to be easygoing? Definitely not. She preferred to have her own way; on other occasions she'd made that abundantly clear to everyone within earshot. Was she just a magnanimous three-year-old? Ha! Are there any?

Whatever the reason, I know enough about children and their whining ways to know a miracle when I see one. If children are ever inclined to make a scene or throw a tantrum, it's in the middle of a crowded mall during a busy lunch hour. As if they know that there are too many witnesses for you to kill them.

The miracle was this: Megan's toy was missing and she had a choice to make. I imagine her thinking, in her own little preschool way, something like this: *My toy is missing. I could kick and scream and throw a tantrum. I could whine and cry and demand a toy for myself. I could steal my brother's toy. Those are all options, but none will change the fact that my toy is missing. So I'll accept the reality of my situation and move on to enjoy what I've got right here in front of me.*

Megan chose wisely.

Good Grief

Don't we all have those times in life when we could say, "My toy is missing"? My mother has lost some of her "toys" over the years (including her marbles, she told me recently). She's lost three husbands and almost all of her nine siblings. Now she's losing her short-term memory and the ability to live independently. Lots of missing toys.

Others know the feeling too. My sister, my aunt, and two friends who are younger than I am are all widows. Another friend miscarried a baby, and then another. And then a third.

We suffer in this life, don't we? Lost loves. Lost health. Lost dreams.

So much sorrow. So much pain. So many missing toys.

And the grieving process—so necessary for our heal-ing—is long and complicated. What Megan covered in mo-ments can take years for us to fully experience as we confront our losses.

We grieve. Anger is certainly part of the grieving process. We kick and scream at the unfairness of life. I've certainly been angry at times, as I've said before. We may, in anger, even raise our fist to heaven and curse at God.

Like Job, we curse the day we were born. "May the day of my birth perish, and the night it was said, 'A boy is born!'" He asks, "Why did I not perish at birth, and die as I came from the womb?" (Job 3:3, 11). Why are we born, he asks, if only to suffer?

Job's "toys"—his children, his property, and his health—were missing. And he suffered. "For sighing comes to me in-stead of food; my groans pour out like water. What I feared has come upon me; what I dreaded has happened to me. I have no peace, no quietness; I have no rest, but only turmoil" (Job 3:24–26). Job was grieving. Job was depressed.

Shock, denial, anger, and depression—all are natural re-sponses to grief. I'm not a medical professional, but I know that depression triggered by a particular event—a loss, a death, a trauma, a major change in life—can, if left unad-dressed, fester into a longer-term depression that requires medical help.

I also know how impossible it is to "Lighten up!" or "Snap out of it!" when we're depressed. No matter how many times others give us that advice. No matter how many times we tell ourselves to do so.

Divorce depressed me. "My marriage is missing" is never a happy thought. Marriages don't come apart easily. God intended that "two shall become one" for life. That bond cannot be broken cleanly. Before the courts ever declare a divorce final, we suffer the stress of a sick and dying relationship, the fighting and the forgiving, the rejections and the reconciliations. All of that takes its emotional toll.

A marriage falling apart feels like this: first you have the toy, and then you don't. Then you have it again. Then it's gone again. You hope, and then the hope is crushed. You dare to hope again, only to be disappointed again. That on-again, off-again pattern is a killer. The "yes, no, maybe so" of a relationship breaking up is emotionally exhausting.

Depression shuts down the feelings. I spent days and weeks in the pits of despair. I stayed in the house with the curtains drawn and the lights off. Each morning, I battled up through the dark cloud that threatened to smother me. I went through the motions of living, because I had little children to care for, while the darkness hovered just there beyond the moment, waiting to swallow me whole if I stopped moving. I needed help.

Have you felt that darkness? Do you feel it today? Get help. Open the curtains. Get help. Let the light in. Get help. God has a better way for you to live. Believe me. Please. Get help. Today.

Denial, anger, depression are all expected as we process our grief over our missing toys. But what about stealing someone else's toy? Envy drives us to do all kinds of things as we grieve. Envy clouds our judgment, and worse. "Envy rots the bones," says Proverbs 14:30. Envy is in the list of the "acts of the sinful nature" detailed in Paul's epistle to the Galatians (5:21).

And James makes it clear that "if you harbor bitter envy and selfish ambition in your hearts, do not boast about it or deny the truth. Such 'wisdom' does not come down from heaven but is earthly, unspiritual, of the devil. For where you have envy and selfish ambition, there you find disorder and every evil practice" (James 3:14–16).

In the case of marital infidelity, stealing someone else's toy is what the world calls having an affair or fooling around. The Bible calls it adultery and makes it clear that "thou shalt not commit" it. Not a suggestion but a commandment.

Stealing someone else's toy is never a good solution. Innocents are hurt. A relationship founded on lies and treachery cannot thrive. How envy twists our lives. Our view is distorted when we focus only on what others have that is missing from our lives.

Acceptance

"There is a time for everything," says the writer of Ecclesiastes (3:1). When our toys are missing, when our joy is taken from us in this life, there is a time to grieve, to rage, to wail, to mourn, and to suffer.

And then, just as certainly, there is a time to accept the reality of our situation and move on. What Megan did in a few moments may take us years. We may require medical or psychological intervention to help us accept our losses and manage our grief.

How long does it take? Nobody can say. It's a process. Every situation is different. Every heart is different. Job, in his misery, was surrounded by friends who felt compelled to "help" him by offering advice.

The least helpful friends are those who say, "Oh, good grief! It's been (whatever number) days (or weeks or months or years). Isn't it time for you to be moving on?" You want to say, "Oh! I'm so sorry! I had no idea my suffering was making you so miserable! You poor darling! I'll get over it right this minute!"

The least helpful friends are those who say, "Cheer up. It could be worse. Think of all those people who would love to be in your position because they never had (whatever it was you lost)." You sigh and hope your friend never has to find out what your position feels like.

The least helpful friends are those who think they can read God's mind and see the future. "This is God's will … This is for the best … You'll have other babies … You'll find someone else …" Must be nice to be so smart, huh?

The least helpful friends may be like Job's wife, who encouraged him in the pits of his despair to "curse God and die!" Sheesh! With friends like that, who needs enemies?

The most helpful friends are just there with you as you grieve. Just there, sharing comfort, filling the emptiness with their presence. They pray for you. They make you tea. They come bearing chocolate. They laugh when you laugh. They cry when you cry. They are simply there, waiting with you for relief, for understanding, and, eventually, for acceptance.

The ultimate acceptance Jesus modeled for us. In the garden. Sweating blood. "Father, if you are willing, take this cup from me; yet not my will, but yours be done" (Luke 22:42). Jesus, suffering in his humanity, acknowledging the sovereignty of the Father. The key to acceptance is surrender to the sovereignty of God.

Job arrived at acceptance, after all the anger, the advice, the debating, the protesting, and the suffering. God asks Job in the end, "Do you send the lightning bolts on their way? Do you know when the mountain goats give birth? Does the eagle soar at your command? Where were you when I laid the earth's foundation?" (See Job, chapters 38 and 39.)

This is sovereignty. This is God.

Our response? Job modeled it for us as he replied to the Lord, "I know that you can do all things; no plan of yours can be thwarted. You asked, 'Who is this that obscures my counsel without knowledge?' Surely I spoke of things I did not understand, things too wonderful for me to know.... My ears had heard of you but now my eyes have seen you. Therefore I despise myself and repent in dust and ashes" (Job 42:1–3, 5–6).

God knows the length and depth of our darkness and grief. God knows the point at which we are ready to accept. We come to the dawn of our acceptance when we sense God asking us, as he asked Job, "Have you ever given orders to the morning, or shown the dawn its place?" We are with Job, echoing his answer as we say, "What was I thinking to question your authority, Lord? Life isn't fair and I don't understand why things happen. But you are God. I am not. I repent in dust and ashes."

We are in the garden, surrendering. "Your will be done."

When your toy is missing, allow yourself the time you need to grieve, however long it takes. God will bring you through it. And then, when the time is right, with the help of God, accept the new reality of your life.

Acceptance is freedom. Freedom from the pain. Freedom from the sorrow.

Acceptance is freedom. Freedom to cherish the warm memories and celebrate the gifts of a new day and a fresh hope.

Acceptance is freedom. Freedom to enjoy your blessings— life, laughter, love, and teddy-bear cookies.

Satisfy us in the morning with your unfailing love,
that we may sing for joy and be glad all our days.
Make us glad for as many days as you have afflicted us,
for as many years as we have seen trouble.
—Psalm 90:14–15

* *

Points to Ponder

1. Make a list of the "missing toys" in your life. Which loss has been most difficult for you?

2. Now make a list of your blessings. Choose one blessing and give thanks. Decide how you can share one of your blessings with someone else. Do it.

3. What are you grieving today? Where are you in the process? Write about your feelings. Spend some time in prayer.

* *

21

Frames

Mother looked at the shelf in her bedroom. "What is that book up there? *On Golden Pond*? What's that book about?" It's not a book at all but a movie she has watched dozens of times. The last time was just a week ago.

"It's a movie, Mom, remember?" I told her, taking it from the shelf. We've repeated this pattern countless times in the past year. She forgets. I give her cues in hopes of triggering memories.

I point at the cover. "See, here is Henry Fonda. He plays the old guy." Mother squints at Henry, trying to put it all together.

I continue filling in her blanks. "And here's Katherine Hepburn. She plays his wife. Remember?" Mother shakes her head.

"Remember what she calls him?" I do my best voice-wavering imitation of the late great Hepburn, "You old poop!'" Mother laughs and then she recognizes the picture of Jane Fonda as well, the real-life daughter playing the movie daughter. She's remembering more and I feel encouraged. "That daughter was always trying to earn her father's love," she says.

"Yes, she was," I agree. I carry *On Golden Pond* across the room to her TV. "Did you want to watch the movie?"

She seems surprised by my offer. "What movie is it?" she asks.

Where are you, Mom? The silent question floats above us so often. Mother is over ninety. She has dementia. She can remember long-ago things, but her brain can't record new information. That's the simplest explanation I've found. The reality of it is this: my mother is here, yet she often is not.

I feel as if I'm looking at a photograph of my mother, a photo that fades a little with each moment like this. The strong mother I used to see, the brave bright woman whose energetic movement filled the frame of life, is diminished daily by this dementia. She is shrinking, physically and mentally, into a frail whisper of herself.

One day, she'll disappear. The frame will be empty.

One thing, however, remains unaltered by time: my mother's laugh, always ready and a joy to hear. Her sense of humor—no question a gift from God—sustains her. It always has. On a recent morning, she laughed as she told me how her dentures—she's worn dentures for over sixty years—slipped out of her hand while she brushed them. "They fell to the floor, bounced out the bathroom door, and skittered down the hall," she laughed. "I guess my teeth had a mind of their own this morning!"

It is so good to laugh with my mother. I am blessed to still have these moments of silly joy with her. But as I laugh, I also mourn for what once was. This is the dichotomy of this season of caregiving, being caught between the opposing forces of holding on and letting go at the same time.

I am a daughter longing for her mother; I am a mother familiar with the pain of letting go.

I miss the conversations we used to have, back when my mother was fully engaged in this life. She lives now in what we call "her reality of the moment."

In her reality, she might be a child again, riding to school in a sleigh down frozen country roads. I hear the bells and the muffled clop of hooves in snow. I see the frosty snorts of horse breath hanging in the still morning.

In another moment, she's waiting, watching, for her older sister to come home from the city, bringing a gift of ice skates. Later she'll skate to school on the frozen river.

In another of her moments, Mother listens to the music as her parents dance at a Saturday night barn dance. How they love to dance. How she loves to watch. I watch with her. Again and again.

In other moments, she's with her siblings applauding her father's acrobatics in the front yard. Was he a gymnast in the old country? She doesn't know. She only remembers how he amazed and astounded the adoring crowd with his tricks. I'm amazed and astounded too.

In a favorite recurring moment, she is very small—maybe seven years old—and sitting in the blacksmith shop watching her father work. "He told me, 'Stay in that corner and don't move or the horse might step on you!'"

Listening to her, I hear the cracking fire, the clang of hammer on metal, the hiss of hot steel meeting water. I smell horse flesh and the young-man sweat of my grandfather at work. I see the little girl huddled against a wood-plank wall. As my mother talks, I sense her little-girl fear mixed with the thrill of being so close to the fire, the heat, and the danger. The thrill and the fear of being in the presence of such power. Of such a father.

And I'm certain she can see it, hear it, and smell it, just as if it were yesterday.

But yesterday she wasn't seven. Yesterday she went to "The Club," an adult day-program where others in similar circumstances—physically challenged, memory impaired, or both—gather to socialize, talk, laugh, and eat together with caring staff members, while we who are family caregivers take advantage of the respite. Yesterday at the Club, she wasn't seven, but an elderly woman who has memory trouble.

What did she do at the club? She doesn't remember. What did she have for lunch? She can't recall. Who was there?

"The Scowler was there, and she scowled at me," Mother says. She's mentioned this woman before, whose face seems frozen in an angry grimace. "She hates me," Mother says. I've suggested that perhaps the woman has a physical ailment or a medication issue that makes her crabby. Mother doesn't think so. "No, she hates me. That's what it is," she insists.

Today, here, she is old and weak and vulnerable to scowlers. Her memories of long ago are saturated with simple pleasure and warm kindness. No wonder she prefers the reality of her own moments to this present suffering.

When her dear brother-in-law Glenn passed away recently, I didn't want to tell her. I didn't want to tell her that her younger sister was now a widow after so many decades of marriage. My mother has known that pain three times. I didn't want to tell her. I didn't want to see my mother cry. (We shouldn't make our mommies cry.)

I dug through old family photos and found a picture of my uncle Glenn, taken on a summer day years ago at the lake home where he and my aunt lived. Glenn stands in his driveway, leaning casually against a car. Next to him are my father and my sister's husband, Don. All three are gone now.

Don looks so young, in his twenties—the age my children are now. My father and Glenn look young too—in their forties, I'd guess. Younger than I am now. They were good men. Gnarly-knuckled, hard-muscled working men. Faithful husbands, loving fathers, and loyal friends. Good men filling the frame of our family's life.

When the picture was snapped, they might have just finished a game of horseshoes, or maybe cribbage. It's what the guys usually did on a summer afternoon at Glenn's, while the women drank coffee, talking and laughing in the screen house, and we children ran wild.

Holding the old picture, I suck in a deep breath and knock on my mother's bedroom door. She is sitting in her chair watching *The Price Is Right*. I sit down on the bed and I tell her the cruel truth—that Glenn is gone and her sister is a widow.

My mother cries. I join her. Afterward we talk.

"Who is left of my family?" She asks me this often. Of the ten children and their spouses, three remain—she and her two youngest sisters. Parents, siblings, and friends are all gone. When she asks me if someone from her past is still living, the answer is almost always no.

At what point do we shut down, unable to bear more grief? How much grief can a human heart absorb? How can my mother stand it?

"You've lost so much ... It's not fair ..." I stumble at consolation, inept at expressing the sorrow of living.

She sits up taller, suddenly my mother again. "You can't dwell on those things," she tells me. "You have to think about happier things."

I came to comfort. I left comforted.

Glimpses

On a recent perfect July afternoon, our six-month-old grandson Joey careens across our wooden deck in his walker. His toes pushing against the deck, he heads for his great-grandmother, flying toward her chair as fast as his fat little legs will propel him. He grins at her as he draws closer. She laughs, raising her sandaled feet in front of her to stop the walker. His forward progress abruptly halted, Joey grabs her toes and, suddenly voracious, lunges as if to gnaw them. My mother squeals in mock protest. Joey squeals right back.

And I look on. In *my* reality of the moment, I worry that the baby will get slivers in his tiny toes. Or that gnawing on her toes will make him sick. I worry that my mother will fall out of her chair, or that she might be getting overheated. I worry that their play has gone on too long, that they both need to nap, or that they both may be getting hungry.

I watch them at play, in another dichotomous moment of delight and dread. In the moments or days or months or years to come—we don't know, for we are not the masters of time—Joey will advance as Mother declines. I will watch the inevitability of both until the moment when time trespasses on happiness—it always does—and grief becomes reality. The frame will be empty.

But that moment is not this moment. "You have to think about happier things," my mother always said. In this momentary reality, as Joey and my mother laugh together, surprise and delight commingle. Nearly a century separates them in age, but it doesn't matter. In this moment, they are mother and child at play.

In this glimpse of heaven, she is young and alive, aware and connected. In this glimpse of heaven, all earthly woes dissipate, carried away on the wings of simple joy.

My mother is teaching me this: I have a choice. I can choose to focus on what was, to lament and mourn my mother's "passing" even before she is gone from this earth. I can bemoan the fact that we cannot have a conversation like we used to, that she cannot move or think like she used to. I can complain and whine to anyone who will listen. I can choose to be consumed by anticipated pain and grief.

I have another choice: to accept what is and move forward, embracing the day as it comes, one small grace at a time. Just as she does.

I can choose to understand and celebrate the fact that life does go on. That the empty frame not only represents what once was, which is something to remember and cherish, but also is open to be filled again, having room now for something new—something to embrace and celebrate.

Life is the process of the frame filling and emptying and filling, again and again and again.

A few nights ago, I brought my mother her bedtime dish of ice cream. She was reading before sleep, propped up in bed against lavender pillows, which set off her pink nightgown and white curls. Framed in the soft light of her bedside lamp, she was the picture of contentment. She smiled at me.

"I forgot to tell you what happened at the Club today," she said. "The Scowler kept trying to say something to me. I told her I couldn't understand her and to talk slow." Mother paused for effect, ever mischievous. "So she looked right at me and said, very slowly, 'You … are … beautiful. And I … love you.'"

This momentary reality, fraught though it is with pain, is also framed, at times, in soft and unexpected grace.

The next morning, my mother woke and told me she'd had a dream in which she walked with her mother. Both of them young, they talked and laughed like good friends as they walked up the big hill in the little town where they used to live. The town where my mother skated and rode in sleighs. Where her father shod horses and dazzled onlookers with his gymnastic prowess. The little town with the big hill where they danced and played and laughed and dreamed.

"Do you suppose it was heaven?" she asked.

Perhaps it was a glimpse of heaven—that place of aliveness and awareness and connection. Where all our suffering is over, where broken hearts are mended, and tears have no place. Where the frame of our desire for unconditional love—a daughter's longing for her father's love—is finally and eternally filled.

Or perhaps heaven is more that place where we sit as children, awestruck and consumed by the thrill of being in the presence of such power, such a Father, and such love.

"Do you suppose it was heaven?" my mother asked me again, smiling. Anticipating.

I don't know, but as my mother talked on, she described it in such vivid detail, it was as if she could see it, hear it, and smell it.

Just as if it were tomorrow.

> Whom have I in heaven but you?
> And earth has nothing I desire besides you.
> My flesh and my heart may fail,
> but God is the strength of my heart
> and my portion forever.
> —Psalm 73:25–26

✳✳✳✳✳✳✳✳✳✳✳✳✳✳✳✳✳✳✳✳✳✳✳✳✳✳✳✳✳✳✳✳✳✳✳✳✳✳

Points to Ponder

1. How forgetful are you? (Some forgetfulness is absolutely normal. I read that somewhere. Don't ask me where.) Describe an embarrassing forgetful moment you've had.

2. What memories are strongest from your childhood? What do you remember seeing, hearing, touching, tasting, and smelling? Which sense memories are strongest for you?

3. Is there an empty frame in your life? Do you have a sense or a hope of the empty frame refilling? How so? Name your feelings and commit it all to God in prayer.

✳✳✳✳✳✳✳✳✳✳✳✳✳✳✳✳✳✳✳✳✳✳✳✳✳✳✳✳✳✳✳✳✳✳✳✳✳✳

22

Seeing

One late March morning, I stood at my kitchen window, and as I waited for the coffeemaker to finish brewing, I grumbled. *Seven inches of new snow. Great.* A sudden drop in temperature had turned last evening's rain to snow overnight. Lots of snow. *Winter's dragged on long enough; I'm ready for spring, Lord. But no ... here's more snow. Ugh.*

Same old same old, I thought. Winter was hanging on like a bad cold. I suffer a touch of seasonal affective disorder at times—that seasonal depression brought on by endless gray, dreary days in certain climates. But even in sunnier places, we can feel like it is winter in those seasons of life when illness, weariness, frustration, or grief drags on and on and on. Just like the dark gray skies of an endless winter.

My mother called to me from her bedroom down the hall from the kitchen. Going to her room, I saw that her roll-up window blind was messed up. Again. It was obvious that the previous night, when she tried to lower the blind, the strings that control the shade had slipped off the edges of the blind. This happened with regular frequency. It was becoming annoying.

The blind hung limp, almost to the floor. *Oh, great. One of my first chores of the day will be blind repair. Again.* I'd have to wrestle the blind free of its hooks and take it down to repair it. I was already cranky; I didn't need to be fixing a stupid window blind before I'd even had coffee.

I took down the blind. The window exposed, my mother looked outside and exclaimed with school-girl delight, "Oh! Look at the snow! Isn't it beautiful? I've never seen *anything* like this!"

My first thought, cranky and evil daughter that I am, was, *Oh, I'm so sure that in over ninety years of living, you've never seen anything like this! I'm sure that in over ninety winters, you've never seen snow like this snow! What's the big deal about this snow, anyway? I'm sick of snow!*

All that raced through my brain, along with the fact that she has failing eyesight due to her glaucoma; she doesn't always see what she thinks she sees. And her failing memory sometimes fools her into thinking the same old thing is a brand new thing. I thought all that even as I said (flatly and with, I'm ashamed to admit, just the *slightest* tinge of sarcasm), "Yes, Mother, it is truly amazing."

I hauled the blind out of her room and into the kitchen. All the frustration of the previous weeks—the cleaning up, the serving, the cooking, the laundry, the fixing, the everything involved in the endless repetition of days and weeks and months of caregiving—weighed suddenly and heavily down on me.

Terry, who was minding his own business at the kitchen table, looked up when I slammed the bundle of blind and strings down on the tabletop. "Something wrong?" he asked. Not much gets past him.

I scowled and then hissed, "I just can't *take* it anymore! I can't take one more *day* of this. I can't take another *minute! I have had it!*"

I left the blind in a tangled heap on the table, stomped out into the sunroom, and flopped down in a wicker chair with a view to the woods. I had one fleeting sarcastic thought along the lines of, *Oh gosh, you poor baby. Any woman who has a sunroom with a view to the woods has no business complaining about how tough her life is.* But I quickly dismissed that latter line of thinking and just focused on the "poor baby" part. (I mean, really, what good is a pity party without the pity?)

In pouting silence, I dared God to cheer me up. I dared him to make me feel better. I was, after all, a long-suffering giver of care; I'd been a mother for over thirty years, and now, with the kids finally grown and freedom within my grasp, I ended up taking care of my aged mother. And I'd been taking care of my recently ailing husband. And I had the house—oh yes, the house with the endless list of things to fix, toilets to scrub, and blinds to restring.

I dismissed another fleeting thought, a thought that didn't have my usual sarcastic bite, which means it might not have come from me. The thought that any woman my age blessed enough to have a husband and children, *and* grandchildren, *and* a comfortable home, and still *have* her mother—*that* woman certainly has no business complaining. But I dismissed the "no business complaining" part because I was, after all, so terribly *burdened* with all my blessings. Poor, poor baby!

I sat and pouted about how God just didn't understand how I was feeling, how frustrated and tired I was. He just didn't seem to realize how sick I was of all of it. Sick of the endless gray in this winter of my life. So I sat and sulked, staring at the stupid woods. In my stupid sunroom. In my stupid life.

A quick breeze blew up a mist of snow, veiling the forest. The breeze passed, the mist settled. Stillness settled over me.

And then I saw it.

Oak, maple, poplar, and pine, all frosted in white magnificence from the base of each trunk to the tippy-tips of the tiniest branches. The forest had been repainted from an infinite palette of shades of gray and white. How could there be so many shades of gray? The dull, dead forest had been recreated in a delightful mosaic, an intricate pattern pieced together against the palest, softest gray of winter sky.

The low-growing brush had looked so scrawny the day before. But now the thorny blackberry brambles, thickened with snow and melded with the stubs of newborn oak and bristly pine babies, looked as dense and unassailable as in high summer.

And above it all and surrounding it all, I sensed the deep winter silence. A silence that falls in moments like this over places like this, places where there is no city clamor—no shouts, no horns, no traffic, no sirens. A thick silence that seems to have substance as it hovers over the forest. No creature disrupts the hush; it would be sacrilege to do so, for this silence is blessed. There is no sound but the one voice, the only voice privileged to speak into it. The one who broke the original silence to create this place, all of it, with his word.

The one who said, "Let there be ..." And it was.

It was. I could see it then, this incredible amazing forest cloaked in late winter snow on a sunless March morning. I could hear it too, imagining the voice of the one who created sky, and trees, and brush, and snow—the very air I breathe. I imagined all of it—sky, trees, brush, snow, and air—joining in concert, with God conducting, to create the music of a new world. A new world of wonder just outside my window.

The veil, like the mist of snow, had been blown aside by holy breath. The veil gone, I could see. Every fraction of every inch of familiar forest looked different. And I knew that I had never seen anything like it. In my fifty-plus years of living, in fifty-plus winters, I'd never seen the likes of this snowy morning.

I couldn't have seen it before, because God had made it new, just this morning.

It was new. And my mother had seen that. How could she have seen so clearly? Not with her eyes, nor with her mind, but only with the accumulated wisdom she's gained in 33,580-plus days of experience. The wisdom of her heart.

Every day is a new day. The prophet Jeremiah wrote, "Because of the LORD's great love we are not consumed, for his compassions never fail. They are new every morning; great is your faithfulness. I say to myself, 'The LORD is my portion; therefore I will wait for him.' The LORD is good to those whose hope is in him, to the one who seeks him" (Lamentations 3:22–25).

God's mercies are new every morning. His steadfast love is shown to us in new mercies each day. My mother pointed me to a new mercy that morning; I was almost too cranky, too angry, too self-pitying, too stubborn, too bitter, and too busy to see it.

Hard-headed, calloused living blinds us to the working of God in our lives. Isaiah carried God's warning, his judgment on those who are "ever hearing, but never understanding; ... ever seeing, but never perceiving. Make the heart of this people calloused; make their ears dull and close their eyes.

Otherwise they might see with their eyes, hear with their ears, understand with their hearts, and turn and be healed" (Isaiah 6:9–10).

The Lord says, "Forget the former things; do not dwell on the past. See, I am doing a new thing! Now it springs up; do you not perceive it? (Isaiah 43:18–19). "See, I am doing a new thing," God says every single morning. Winter, spring, summer, or fall. Hot or cold. Sunshine or rain or snow. He is always, every morning, doing a "new thing." My mother was sharp enough to spot it.

Someday, when I grow up, I pray I'll be as sharp as she is.

"See, I am doing a new thing," God says, even as the sameness of life is wearing us down. Even as the winter of our discontent drags on and on and on. Even as the pain continues, the loneliness goes on and the grief refuses to leave. "See, I am doing a new thing," God says, offering a specific promise: "I am making a way in the desert and streams in the wasteland" (Isaiah 43:19).

We must open our eyes! We must believe. We must trust his promise until that day when we wake up and see something we've never seen before. The path through the desert. The stream in the wasteland. The mercy of deliverance, or if not deliverance, then renewed strength to endure. We must open our eyes to the bright shining hope that God *is* good to those who wait for him, to those who seek him.

Meanwhile, back in the sunroom, I ask, *Now what? What am I to do on this glorious gray-white mosaic of a winter's day?* I know the answer. I make up my mind to do what I've been called to do, on days like this and on sun-brightened July days and on rainy days in May. Every day for this season of life.

Fix the blind. Scrub the toilet. Wash the clothes. Cook the meals. Tell my mother I'm sorry I was so cranky. Thank my husband for understanding, again. Serve. Love. Care. Tell that sarcastic cranky woman living in my head to keep quiet while I thank the Lord that I *have* the "burden of my blessings." Ask God to help me bear my blessings with good humor.

Ask him for mercy, strength, and compassion. Ask him for love, peace, patience, and kindness. Ask him for faithfulness, gentleness, and self-control. Be grateful that I'm needed, and grateful I have people to love. And find, in that, my joy.

And in the middle of it all, to be a witness, to pay close attention, and to take notes. And later, to write about it.

I am a witness, writing to tell you what I saw with my own eyes on one gloriously snowy morning in early spring, when God parted the veil and allowed me to behold his hand at work.

"What do you want me to do for you?" he [Jesus] asked.
"Lord," they answered, "we want our sight."
Jesus had compassion on them and touched their eyes.
Immediately they received their sight and followed him.
—Matthew 20:32–34

✳✳✳

Points to Ponder

1. Describe the season of life you are in right now. What is the biggest challenge? What is the greatest blessing of this season?

2. What "new thing" are you trusting God for today? What helps you to keep believing?

3. If Jesus asked, "What do you want me to do for you?" how would you answer? How do you hope he would respond?

✳✳✳

23

I Will Pass This Way but Once

Time flies when you're having fun. Time's a-wastin'! Time drags. Time marches on. Time heals all wounds, and wounds all heels, some say.

Groucho Marx said, "Time flies like an arrow. Fruit flies like a banana."

What is time? Time is artificial, a man-created thing to help us handle life, to give us an illusion of control. Without the artificial construct we call time, we would explode.

The Bible describes a "day" in Genesis. The beginning and the end of the first day, and the second, and so forth. It's impossible to know how long each day was in the beginning. Did God need twenty-four of our hours to create each day's results? Would God need more than the first millisecond to bring forth the light from the darkness? I don't think so. But what does it matter? "In the beginning, God created" is all that really counts. In the beginning, he was. "Before the mountains were born or you brought forth the earth and the world, from everlasting to everlasting you are God" (Psalm 90:2).

But what is time, really? What is a day? A day of joy can seem to race on, a whirl of laughter and song. A day of pain ticks by, agonizing second by agonizing second. I believe what I heard the other day: time is an emotion. Think about it. Time speeds up when good things are happening. Time drags on and on when you are in the hospital waiting room.

Time drags when you are checking the mailbox daily for the letter from a loved one far away. Time races on vacation. Time drags when you are all dressed, waiting for your prom date to show up. Time flies once you get to the prom. Time is suspended in certain moments. A first kiss. Love walking toward you, home at last. Waiting for the baby's first cry.

Does time really change? Of course not. A minute is still a minute, an hour still an hour. But the feeling changes. What time is it for you, right now? Is time dragging on as you wait and worry? Is it racing by in the rush of a thousand blessings? Time is a mix of dread and delight, anxiety and eager anticipation.

Time is life.

God is not bound by our time; he exists and operates outside our time-space continuum. The psalmist writes, "For a thousand years in your sight are like a day that has just gone by, or like a watch in the night" (Psalm 90:4). It's hard to imagine one who is not constrained by time and space as we are.

What would it be like to see all and know all, all of time, all at once? To see the beginning and the end of the story at the same time? To know what has already been and what is coming, and yet allow for the players in the story to exercise free will, knowing what all their options are—you've assigned them, after all—and letting them choose, and then coordinating the entire production so that it concludes according to your plan. What an amazing author, stage manager, director, and producer you'd have to be. What an amazing Creator God he is.

What does that fact of God have to do with my time right here, right now? God knows where I came from. God knows where I've been. "Your eyes saw my unformed body. All the days ordained for me were written in your book before one of them came to be" (Psalm 139:16).

God knows where I am, right now—what I'm feeling, dreaming, and worrying about. God knows where I'm heading, knows the future, and has a plan. " 'For I know the plans I have for you,' declares the LORD, 'plans to prosper you and not to harm you, plans to give you hope and a future' " (Jeremiah 29:11).

What am I worried about then? My time is in his hands.

Twilight Song

My parents loved to sing; I learned the songs of their generation as a child. Mother and I sang an old, old song together as I did her hair one morning. She sat at the kitchen table with her coffee, while I pressed the hot curling iron into sections of her white hair, twisted the rod and released, again and again, sectioning, pressing, twisting, releasing as we sang:

> *Just a song at twilight, when the lights are low,*
> *and the flickering shadows softly come and go,*
> *though the heart be weary, sad the day and long,*
> *still to us at twilight comes love's old song,*
> *comes love's old sweet song.*

We are together in this time, in this season—my mother's twilight. I am so grateful for this time together, even as I listen to the stories she's told me a dozen times or more. She asks me questions she's known the answer to for decades, as if she's never thought of these things before. Time has little meaning for her anymore. Tuesday is Saturday is Wednesday. We sang the song yesterday or last week or thirty years ago. Time matters not.

Looking at the vase on the kitchen table, she asked again that morning, as she'd asked yesterday and the day before, and the day before that. "What happened to your roses?" The beautiful white roses Terry brought home almost two weeks before had wilted. Still in the vase, they'd dried out, heads drooping and petals dropping rapidly. They needed to be thrown out, but I'd just not done it. And each time Mother asked, "What happened to your roses?" she seemed freshly disappointed that roses don't last forever.

Roses don't last forever. Nothing does in this world.

One recent night, we sat in her room, looking at an old family group photo. In the picture, she and her siblings, along with their husbands and wives, surround her mother, my grandmother. She thinks—but can't be sure—they all were gathered for their mother's birthday. Seventeen people in all.

"Who is still living?" She asks me this often. Only she and a younger sister remain. I told her the truth. A wave of fresh grief—people don't last forever—passed across her face.

Hoping to change the subject, I pointed to my father in the picture. "There's my daddy," I said, searching for common cheerier ground. A confusion of past and present crossed her face. She furrowed her brow, stared intently at me, and asked, "Whose kid are you?"

I was dumbstruck. She repeated the question. "Whose kid are you?"

The little girl in me fought tears—such a question for a mother to ask her child! Then the caregiver took over—a reasonable question for an old woman trying to piece together the fragments of memory tumbling through her brain. The poor dear's been married three times, after all. My older sister is the product of the first marriage; my two brothers and I the product of the second marriage, to the man in the picture. She had a third man; they had no children but a lot of fun. (Hmm. Is there a connection there?)

So many years. So many faces. So many names. Trying to put it all together in the context of time is difficult at her age. (At *my* age!) I understood all that, and yet ...

Later, alone, I cried out to God. *Whose kid* am *I?* I cried out the heartache of watching my mother slip away from me, from this time and this place. The day is coming, sooner rather than later, when she will not recognize me. The day is coming, sooner rather than later, when she will be gone. I know. I know. Mothers don't last forever.

Separation is part of life. We take a first independent step, then in a moment, it seems, we're off to school. In no time, we're grown and gone. That's life. And those separations are celebrated. Childhood isn't supposed to last forever. Children grow up. That's the way it is supposed to be. Parents age and die. Time moves on.

"Whose kid are you?" felt like abandonment, rejection, and crueler than death: the parent who doesn't know you anymore lives to remind you of that fact every day. The caregiver knows it's the disease; the child cries.

We exist together in this temporary state of being, a limbo of strangers who spark some vague and distant flicker of recognition that is gone as quickly as it came — a spark too weak to become flame. A memory thin as a whiff of wood smoke on a gray winter afternoon, suspended for a moment and then swept off with a chill breeze. And afterward, emptiness. Eventually no common ground will remain, no basis for the old relationship. No way to build a new one. No certainty from one day to the next who she will be or who we will be together—mother and child, or child and mother.

"Whose kid are you?" Whose child are we? If we are no longer the child of our parents, then who are we? My mother asked, "Whose kid are you?" and with the sorrow of hearing the question, I also sense a movement forward. I am getting ready to let go, to no longer be the child of my earthly parents—we earthly parents are only temporary caretakers, after all. I am, and will remain forever, who I truly am: a daughter of the King.

"Whose kid are you?" sparks a turning point in my life. I've come into my own. This feels like spiritual adulthood, which is ironic since I am God's "child," but the parenthood of God is eternal, transcending this temporal relationship of earthly biological parent and child. Today I transcend this plane of existence and assume, in a new way, my true citizenship in the kingdom of heaven. Today I see in a new way that God is my Father, my true Parent, and I am *his* child. Forever.

Whose kid am I? I am a child of God. I'm ready to let go. It's time.

Time

We pass through the temporal—these moments, days, weeks, and years of life on this earth. How do we live? We have a choice. We can choose to pass through life, grasping at each moment, packing as much activity and distraction into each day as our calendar will hold. We can choose to pass through life clutching our entitlements to our bosom, even as we claw for more; hanging on for all we're worth to people or possessions, afraid of who we will be if we let go. We can choose to pass through life holding on to the past or the pain, the resentment or the anger, because release and healing are, we tell ourselves, just too hard.

Or we can realize that nothing lasts in this world—not roses, not relationships—and choose to hold loosely to the things of this earth. It's our choice. We will pass this way but once.

I will pass this way but once. Let me therefore pay attention to the moments that matter—moments of tender connection with other travelers.

I will pass this way but once. Let me therefore give myself time to enjoy the journey. Time to laugh and play. Time to untwist. Time to eat, exercise, and sleep. Time to unwind. Time to reflect. Time to grieve. Time to accept. Time to heal. Time to get ready to move forward.

Time in God's company. I will pass this way but once. Let me therefore live purposefully, in prayer, so that I may be equipped and empowered by God to do that for which he has given me life. Spending my days—my moments—doing what really matters: loving and serving others in his name.

I will pass this way but once. Let me therefore release quickly those encumbrances that would stop my forward progress. Letting go of anger, resentment, entitlement, and self. Seeking peace, finding forgiveness, and learning to forgive. Learning to give.

I will pass this way but once. Let me live this life, one grace-filled moment to the next, with my eyes fixed on Jesus, knowing—certain—that everything that really matters is just fine. That despite the ups and downs, the twists and the trials, God has everything in his hands, and there is a time and a purpose for everything.

I stepped outside the other night, after dinner. The sun had just set; the world glowed softly in its last light. I breathed in the warm, late-summer evening air.

Twilight time.

I exhaled and released my worries—the money, health, and family issues that had been on my mind through the busy day—to God. "This is good," I said. "This is good."

That "life I ordered" fairy tale never came true. Real life—the Twister life—has been so much better than that. Not easy, but so much better.

Better, in spite of the twistings and knots. Better, in spite of bad hair days, financial troubles, and strong-willed challenges. Better, in spite of divorce, wedding stress, and Alzheimer's. Better, in spite of vet bills, hospital bills, mice in the attic, and bats in the belfry. Better, in spite of traffic jams, things that leak, and things that sag.

In real life, through the testing, the twisting, the trials, and the troubles—whether they are coming, going, or with us—we learn how very real God is, and how very much he loves us.

In real life, through the hassles, headaches, and heartaches, we laugh, cry, and pray. We may beg, wheedle, and cajole. Deny, bargain, and rage. Whine, sob, and surrender. And in the end, because God loves us, we stand.

We stand on the promises of the one who never changes, never forsakes us, and never fails us. We stand by faith—and even that is his gift to us—in the one who has everything we need to make it through. The one who has given us the treasure of his Spirit, inhabiting our fragile humble hearts. "We have this treasure in jars of clay to show that this all-surpassing power is from God and not from us" (2 Corinthians 4:7).

We stand because we learn that in the middle of the troubles, the trials, and the twisting, God is there. God cares.

His promise is not for a life of ease but for a life of endurance. "We are hard pressed on every side, but not crushed; perplexed, but not in despair; persecuted, but not abandoned; struck down, but not destroyed" (2 Corinthians 4:8–9).

In real life, we have troubles that press hard on us, dogging and confounding us, and at times, laying us low. But in the end, we are not crushed, not in despair, not abandoned, and not destroyed. Because God loves us. And in his strength we stand.

We stand in the strength of the one who spoke it all into being. Despite appearances, he has everything in his hands, everything under control. And he loves us.

God, who orders the dawn, provides new mercy for each day. He loves us.

And God, who ordains the twilight, sings us a love song and watches over us as we sleep. He loves us.

God loves us. God cares. And because of that fact, everything that matters in this life, and in the next, is going to be fine. Just fine.

Whatever time it is for you, whatever season it is in your life, God loves you. Though your heart may be weary, though your days may be long, still to you at twilight or at dawn— whatever time it is in your life—comes God's love song. Comes God's old, sweet song.

I have loved you with an everlasting love ... Trust in me ... My peace I give to you ... Come to me ... Come to me ... Come to me ...

I lift up my eyes to the hills—
where does my help come from?
My help comes from the LORD,
the Maker of heaven and earth.
—Psalm 121:1–2

When Did I Stop Being Barbie and Become Mrs. Potato Head?

Learning to Embrace the Woman You've Become

Mary Pierce

Embrace Your Inner Mrs. Potato Head!

She's so much more real and full of fun than Barbie ever could be. And she knows how to laugh like only those who have discovered the humor, heart, and wisdom of true womanhood can laugh. Give her room to romp with this hilarious collection of zany, true-life stories by Mary Pierce.

If you love to kick off your shoes and laugh your socks off over the foibles and absurdities of life, this book is for you. Mrs. Potato Head's hormones are out of whack. Her memory is held together by sticky notes. But she's got a sense of humor that just won't quit, and she's learned to accept and enjoy herself as she is — because God does.

Softcover 0-310-24856-6

Pick up a copy today at your favorite bookstore!

Confessions of a Prayer Wimp

My Fumbling, Faltering Foibles in Faith

Mary Pierce

Is your spiritual life more like a fast-food run than an intimate dinner for two?

Whether it's the busy mother's wish to be Wonder Woman — minus the metal bra — or battles with an exploding hot water heater, or fighting the "Resolutionary War" of New Year's Day, Mary Pierce understands the dilemmas of being a woman in today's 24/7 world. From disorganized misery to extreme organizational mania (she used to refer to her children by their household chores: Cat Box Boy, Dishwasher Girl, and Garbage Can Baby), Pierce deals with our fumbling attempts to grow closer to God, encouraging us as she invites us to laugh, cry, love, embrace life, and pray!

In her humorous, conversational style, Pierce laughs at her mistakes and her prayers that seem more like advertising jingles (Lord, I need a break today, and Can you hear me now, Lord?). In *Confessions of a Prayer Wimp*, you'll come to understand that faith is less about what you are or do or say, and more about who God is—someone who loves you no matter what you do.

Softcover 0-310-24979-1

Pick up a copy today at your favorite bookstore!

We want to hear from you. Please send your comments about this book to us in care of zreview@zondervan.com. Thank you.

ZONDERVAN.com/
AUTHORTRACKER
follow your favorite authors